The War
for
Independence

The War for Independen

THE CHICAGO HISTORY OF AMERICAN CIVILIZAT

Daniel J. Boorstin, EDITOR

Military History

By Howard H. Peckham

THE UNIVERSITY OF CHICAGO PRESS

CHICAGO & LONDON

Library of Congress Catalog Card Number: 58-5685

THE UNIVERSITY OF CHICAGO PRESS, CHICAGO & LONDON
The University of Toronto Press, Toronto 5, Canada

Their virtues shall not only be celebrated by inscriptions on stone in their own country, but abide in the memory of other men in all lands.

From PERICLES' *funeral oration over the Athenian warriors, as reported by Thucydides*

Northern Theater of War

scale of miles

10 20 30 40 50   100

map by Thomas B. Coates

Southern
Theater
of War

map by Thomas Coates

Editor's Preface

In the earlier years of this century, the so-called New History, which turned away from the battlefield to study the market place, the household, and the factory, fostered the misconception that military history is somehow less significant or less expressive of the national culture than other kinds of history. Military events were thought to be outside the main stream of American life. Since we are not a warlike people, we seem to have been afraid that studying wars would foster a bellicose spirit. But in this volume Mr. Peckham shows us how wrong these notions are. His task has been difficult, because the leading military events of the Revolution have been dulled by patriotic familiarity. Mr. Peckham's intimacy with the documents of the war has enabled him to rescue Lexington, Concord, Bunker Hill, and "Washington Crossing the Delaware" from the dull gray of schoolroom engravings and to give them sharp outline and warm color.

We, like other peoples, have been distinguished as much by how we have fought as by what we have fought for. The American Revolution was in many ways a characteristically American war. Unlike earlier European wars, it was not fought

Editor's Preface

primarily by professional soldiers recruited from the taverns, nor was it generaled by a coterie of aristocrats. It was fought mostly by amateurs—citizens in arms—defending their homes; and it revealed many of the advantages and weaknesses of amateur generals. Command and supply were both part of the problem of home rule, which later would become the problem of American federalism. By suggesting these and many other connections between the military and the political and social aspects of our history, Mr. Peckham keeps us in the main stream of American civilization.

This is a short story of a prolonged and far-flung conflict. The War for Independence, lasting for eight years, was twice as long as any of our later wars. Every region east of the Mississippi saw military engagements and some bloodshed; colonial capitals were occupied by the enemy. Mr. Peckham has had to be selective, and much of the value of his volume lies in the dramatic skill with which he has recounted crucial episodes. He gives us a vivid sense of the tension and the smoke of battlefields.

The "Chicago History of American Civilization" aims to make each aspect of our culture a window to all our history. The series contains two kinds of books: a *chronological* group, which provides a coherent narrative of American history from its beginning to the present day, and a *topical* group, which deals with the history of varied and significant aspects of American life. This book is one of the topical group. Other aspects of the story of the struggle for American independence will be found in Edmund S. Morgan's *Birth of the Republic: 1763–89.*

DANIEL J. BOORSTIN

Table of Contents

Prelude to Battle

In 1763 Great Britain, which had just overwhelmed her principal rival empire, the French, in the Seven Years' War, found herself with a huge war debt, additional territories to administer, and an ambitious new king anxious to rule as well as reign. His ministers saw no alternative to laying taxes on the colonies, which existed, according to the imperial view, for the benefit of the mother country.

For a hundred and fifty years after 1607, the American colonies had enjoyed unusual freedom to manage their own affairs —political, religious, commercial, and social. This was not so much a freedom granted by the British government (although Connecticut and Rhode Island had been given charters that permitted much self-government), and certainly not guaranteed by it, as a freedom that accrued from England's preoccupation at home with local interests, from indifference, distance, and inefficiency, or from what Edmund Burke once called "the beneficent negligence of government."

The immediate and tumultuous objection of the Americans to the new taxes puzzled and angered the home government. The American position was that, while Parliament could legislate for the colonies, taxes were a gift to government from the people and could be levied only through their direct representatives—of which they had none in Parliament. Some British Whigs agreed with this novel argument. To get around direct taxation, then, the ministry tried making the colonists pay duties on certain items they imported, since it was acknowledged that Parliament could regulate trade. When the Americans refused to import those goods so as to avoid the duties, Britain sent troops to protect the customs collectors and those merchants who might be willing to accept imports against mob threats.

Seeing that American revenue would be used to pay governors and judges (who had hitherto been dependent on provincial assemblies for their salaries) and viewing the presence of the military as a threat to their civil liberties as Englishmen, objecting colonists advanced their argument another step by questioning the right of Parliament to legislate for them at all. The ministry retreated, not from agreement with the Americans but from practicality (the duties were not producing enough revenue), and repealed all the duties except the one on tea. This exception, which was made to preserve the legal supremacy of Parliament, led to mob action against a cargo of tea in Boston harbor in December, 1773. Parliament retaliated by closing the port to all commerce, suspending the Massachusetts charter, and enacting other coercive measures.

The Americans now asserted their equality: they said that their colonial assemblies stood on equal footing with Parliament and alone could legislate for the colonies, while Parliament legislated for Great Britain. All were united only by loyalty to the Crown. This is the concept today in the British Commonwealth of Nations, but then it was so far in advance of its time as to be inadmissible. A Continental Congress was called to meet at Philadelphia in September, 1774, to consider protests and defensive policies. "The Revolution," John Adams wrote long afterward, "was in the minds and hearts of the people, and in the union of the colonies; both of which were substantially effected before hostilities commenced."

Throughout 1775 most Americans still considered themselves loyal subjects of King George III engaged in resisting a "ministerial army" backed by a Parliament that had exceeded its authority. Early the next year Thomas Paine demolished even this toe hold on the empire ladder by pointing out that the King did not stand neutrally above Parliament but agreed with his ministers; indeed, he had urged on them the measures they had taken. So, arguing that the rights they asserted for themselves were natural and inalienable rights (this from John Locke's late seventeenth-century thought), which a hereditary monarch would always oppose because its basis was usurpation (this from Paine), the Americans took the final and inevitable plunge of declaring themselves in July, 1776, independent of all British connection.

Thus in a decade the Americans developed a political theory in opposition to British imperialism that led them step by step to independence. Perhaps the ultimate issue surprised them, for it was in a sense a discovery at the end of a long search or, intellectually, the resolution of an involved syllogism. It was also a defense of many freedoms they already enjoyed. The goal might still have been denied them by force, and therefore they turned from an appeal to reason to an appeal to arms. The War for Independence was the climax to the argument. It tested the reasoning that had been followed by staking life and property on a vision of how society should be ordered.

This narrative is concerned with showing how an embattled idea triumphed over the repressive might of an outworn concept of government. Because it is military history, it passes over the political, diplomatic, and social developments during the years 1775 to 1783. Rather, it is an account of campaigns and battles, expeditions and sieges, generals and ranks—the war of action and the war of attrition—attempting to make clear not only how the separate colonies managed to carry on such a struggle but also why they won.

It was a small war, perhaps, as wars have come to be fought. Seldom did either army exceed the size of one or two modern divisions. The populations were small, too—two and a half million in the thirteen colonies against nine million in Great Britain. It was a war in which individual courage and skill and perseverance counted heavily. It was a war in which generals led their troops in person. Yet it was a war fought over an immense battlefield, ranging from Quebec to Savannah, from Boston to Vincennes. Soldiers by avocation and reluctant ones, the colonials fought professional troops, career officers, and hired mercenaries. If most of the Americans had some familiarity with muskets and many were used to living in the open, they had no liking for drill or discipline. They may have swallowed propaganda at times that magnified the enemy's cruelty and distorted his intentions, but they were remarkably clear-headed about their rights as citizens. They had positive ideas about the desirability of self-government, religious toleration, an untrammeled press, freedom of trade, and westward expansion. If this is our heritage, it is important to know what it cost, for then we shall remember how highly it was valued by those who secured it.

Moreover, the American Revolution charted our course for the future. We have deviated little from the principles expressed then. We continually turn back to the Revolution to renew our faith in ourselves and to resight our objectives. "It is the tale of the thing done," says Historian George M. Trevelyan, "which trains the political judgment by widening the range of sympathy and deepening the approval or disapproval of conscience; that stimulates by example youth to aspire and age to endure; that enables us by the light of what men once have been, to see the thing we are and dimly to descry the form of what we should be."

The Revolutionary generation set a shining example to the world. It crumbled the Spanish Empire, inspired several national revolutions, forced liberal reforms in England, and gave hope to all repressed peoples. According to Tom Paine, the American Revolution "contributed more to enlighten the world, and diffuse a spirit of freedom and liberality among mankind, than any human event (if this may be called one) that ever preceded it."

For a century and a half the story of the Revolution was a frequent topic of Fourth of July orations delivered in the open under sunny skies. In truth, it should be a winter's tale, told around a hearth on a windy night when there are no distractions, when images rise easily in the flames, the crackling of logs suggests musket shots, and the comfortable warmth is enjoyed as a dividend of that remote victory. It began in Boston, a tense and restless city of sixteen thousand, its business activity stagnated. General Thomas Gage, commander-in-chief of the British forces in North America, also had been named governor of Massachusetts in 1774. He had moved his headquarters to Boston, where he sat in embarrassment with nearly four thousand troops to police the city. He could find few councilors willing to help him govern, and the elected assembly now called itself the Provincial Congress and met illegally elsewhere in defiance of his authority. Other colonies were giving support to obstreperous Massachusetts. A gloomy bitter winter had passed. Now, with springtime . . .

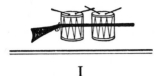

I

"A Middling Force"

The answer had come at long last, and now the decision was to be made.

Thomas Gage, commander-in-chief of His Majesty's Forces in North America and governor of Massachusetts Bay colony, must draw up the orders his patience and good will had postponed and his administrative sense still detested. Parliament had declared Massachusetts to be in a state of rebellion, and the government had made up its mind to use coercion. The letter from Lord Dartmouth, Secretary of State, was explicit:

The only consideration that remains is, in what manner the Force under your command may be exerted. . . . the first essential step to be taken towards re-establishing Government, would be to arrest and imprison the principal Actors and Abettors in the Provincial Congress. . . . any efforts of the people, unprepared to encounter with a regular Force, cannot be very formidable, and tho' such a proceeding should be, according to your idea of it, a signal for hostilities yet . . . it will surely be better that the Conflict should be brought on, upon such ground, than in a riper state of Rebellion.

The suggestion that he seize the rebel leaders Gage rejected on the good ground that, except for Dr. Joseph Warren, they were out of Boston and in hiding. Dartmouth's easy summary did not reflect Gage's careful judgment of the situation in America. He had written earlier to the Secretary at War, Lord Barrington, with bluntness:

> If you will resist and not yield, that Resistance should be effectual at the Beginning. If you think ten thousand men sufficient, send twenty, if one million is thought enough, give two; you will save both Blood and Treasure in the end. A large Force will terrify, and engage many to join you, a middling one will encourage Resistance and gain no friends.

Gage had no way of knowing that his recommendation for use of maximum force had only antagonized the King and his ministers. It was not what they wished to hear, and therefore they imputed it to the general's incompetence, caution, and conciliatory nature. The only concession to the views of the fifty-six-year-old Gage, who had been for twenty years resident in America and had married an American, was Dartmouth's promise that reinforcements would be coming—though not before Gage had to thrust out of Boston and deliver the stroke he well knew would mean war.

In preparation he had alerted the elite companies of each regiment, gathered up boats, and closed the town to exit. Giving himself another couple of days to think it over, Gage studied his spies' reports of the military supplies gathered by the rebels out in Concord, where the Provincial Congress met. Then he took up his quill and began writing to Lieutenant Colonel Francis Smith:

> Sir: You will march with the corps of Grenadiers and Light Infantry put under your command with the utmost expedition and secrecy to Concord, where you will seize and destroy all the artillery and ammunition you can find....

"A Middling Force"

It was the eighteenth of April, 1775. The armed truce in Massachusetts was rapidly coming to an end. The commitment was made.

At ten o'clock that night the expeditionary force began moving out of Boston by boats across Back Bay. Whatever secrecy it once enjoyed had been lost. Loyalists (those who remained loyal to British authority) and rebels alike knew a march was to be made, and the destination could be guessed. The immediate problem for the rebels was to get the news out of the guarded city to their leaders in Concord. When Dr. Warren saw the embarkation begin, he summoned William Dawes and Paul Revere, dispatch riders for the Massachusetts Committee of Correspondence, and sent them off to warn John Hancock, Samuel Adams, and the people generally of their danger. Dawes slipped through the guard across the neck of land that led to Roxbury, then turned his horse northward past Cambridge to the Lexington road. Revere was rowed across the Charles River mouth under the guns of a British man-of-war to Charlestown. There he borrowed a horse and took off for Lexington, sixteen miles distant, which he reached at midnight. Hancock and Adams were routed out of bed. Soon Dawes joined them. The two riders pressed on toward Concord, arousing the farmers along the way.

The marching redcoats began to hear church bells and signal guns and saw the darkness dotted by squares of yellow light in scattered rural windows. Colonel Smith knew there would be no surprise—unless it was for him. He ordered Major John Pitcairn ahead with six companies of light infantry, lightly armed and fast, to secure the bridges over the Concord River. He kept the grenadiers, the tallest and ablest soldiers. His wisest decision, however, was to send news back to Gage and ask for reinforcements.

Just after sunrise on April 19, Pitcairn reached Lexington and found drawn up on the misty village green some seventy Minute Men, the shock troops of the colonial militia organized with the blessing of the Provincial Congress. They did not block the road but stood back on the green in mute protest, making a show of arms. After ordering his own men not to fire, Pitcairn turned them on to the green and demanded that the Minute Men drop their guns and disperse. Their commander, Captain John Parker, a veteran of the French and Indian War, assessed his disadvantage and told his men to withdraw. As they started to move off, Pitcairn (he said later) turned to his own troops to order them to disarm the Minute Men. Then someone's musket flashed in the pan. Whose it was never has been known, and from which side the harmless boom came has been hotly disputed. The signal drew several scattered shots from the British, and then a volley slammed out on the retreating rebels. Several fell; a few doggedly stood their ground and returned the fire. Pitcairn shouted to his men to cease fire, but the officers could not restrain the soldiers. Eight Americans died, and ten were wounded before the redcoats could be got back in marching order, cheering now. Their only casualties were one comrade wounded and Pitcairn's horse hit. The skirmish had not delayed them more than fifteen minutes. Little did any one of them suspect that before nightfall they would pay many times over for the blood they had rashly spilled.

At Concord, six miles beyond, more rebel militia had assembled, but they withdrew across the river, and the British entered the town without resistance about eight o'clock. They set to work searching for arms and supplies, although much had been carted away before dawn. While they burned gun carriages and destroyed flour, they paid for their own food and drink and did not molest the seething inhabitants beyond swearing at a few of them. The suburban militia finally made an attempt to return to town and take the North Bridge. Here the British definitely fired first and killed two men. The rebels then opened up and killed three redcoats and wounded nine. This exchange lasted probably five minutes.

At noon Colonel Smith considered his mission accomplished. He started his men on their return march to Boston, but found his trouble just beginning. All morning the nearby towns had turned out their militia and Minute Men companies to converge on Concord and Lexington. The solid lines of marching redcoats presented wonderful targets which they could fire on at will from behind trees, rocks, or the stone walls that bordered much of the road. The British not only considered this Indian-style sniping unfair and resented it, they were caught at a harrowing disadvantage. Their fear mounted until, within sight of Lexington, they broke into a run. To their joyful relief they fled into the sheltering lines of a heavy reinforcement —about nine hundred men and two cannon under Lord Hugh Percy.

After a half-hour rest the march was resumed. The rebels took up their potshotting again. Percy ordered flanking parties out to keep the enemy at a distance and frequently had to use his field pieces to break up militia concentrations. Nevertheless, the road became a bloody chute all the way to Charlestown, where dusk ended the mauling. Under cover of night and the British warships, the exhausted soldiers were transported into Boston. They had lost 70 men killed, 165 wounded, and 26 missing, in addition to their 13 earlier casualties—a total of 274.

The War for Independence

Rebel Americans to the number of perhaps thirty-five hundred had been involved at various times in the day's engagements. Casualties in dead, wounded, and missing amounted to ninety-three, a gratifyingly small number in contrast to the British loss but an immediate shock to the communities affected. Then the people rebounded with dangerous enthusiasm over their military success against the best the British could send against them. Now they would push the arrogant lobsterbacks into the sea! The Massachusetts Provincial Congress met on April 22 and authorized the raising of thirteen thousand, six hundred Massachusetts troops under General Artemus Ward, an aloof and unhealthy veteran of the French and Indian War. Rhode Island promised fifteen hundred men, Connecticut called for six thousand, and New Hampshire decided to raise two thousand. A New England army—miscellaneous, poorly organized, and quarrelsome—gathered quickly around Boston and started a ring of siege works to reduce the enemy.

All of Gage's worst fears had been realized. The bloodletting had aroused rather than subdued the rebels. British arms, if not disgraced, had at least brought no glory to the King. An ill-trained yet formidable mob of troops formed a barbed arc around Boston from shore to shore and virtually immobilized the heaviest concentration of royal soldiers in North America. Never had a war, which neither side was ready to call by that name, so swiftly become a stalemate.

THE BRITISH ARMY

Britain had emerged in 1763 from the Seven Years' War as the most powerful empire in Europe and maintained a regular army that now totaled almost forty-nine thousand officers and men, of which eighty-five hundred were in America. Gage had with him in Boston less than four thousand. Regiments were small by modern terms, numbering on paper about 475 and each divided into ten companies, two of them called "light infantry" and "grenadiers" and containing the best troops. Rarely, however, was a regiment at full strength; it usually totaled 325 to 400 on duty. Each company of 25 to 38 men was officered by a captain, a lieutenant, an ensign, two sergeants, three corporals, and a drummer. The regiment was commanded by a colonel (or by a lieutenant colonel in his absence) and had a major, a surgeon, a surgeon's mate, and sometimes a chaplain. Officers' commissions were ordinarily obtained by purchase, and a vacancy was offered to the eldest officer in the rank below. If he could not afford the high fee, the next eldest officer was given the chance. Younger sons of titled families usually bought in as ensigns and moved up by purchase as vacancies occurred. Merit seldom had anything to do with promotion, except in occasional instances of battlefield brilliance, and the gulf between privates and officers was almost unbridgeable.

The common weapon was a smoothbore musket, popularly called "Brown Bess." It was of flintlock action, weighed fourteen pounds, and had a barrel forty-four inches long and three-fourths of an inch in diameter. A bayonet extended fourteen inches beyond the muzzle. The cartridge was a paper cylinder containing a lead ball and loose powder; these bullets were carried in a cartouche box suspended from a white strap over the shoulder. (Another strap for holding a canteen crossed from the other shoulder.) One end of the paper cartridge was bitten off and a few grains of powder shaken into the firing pan, which the flint would ignite; the remaining powder was poured down the barrel and the bullet and empty paper rammed in after it. Firing was done in unison by platoons, the men standing in rows two or three deep. They "leveled" their muskets but otherwise took little aim, assuming that some of the bullets from the volley would hit something. Platoons were ordered as close to the enemy as possible before being allowed to fire. The danger came while reloading; therefore the first firing had to be effective, and sometimes it was followed by a bayonet charge rather than a second volley.

Artillery was organized into battalions made up of eight companies, each of 116 officers and men. Cavalry regiments consisted of six troops of 231 each. Engineers, barely recognized as a department, directed siege operations, bridge and fort building, and map making. Intelligence or spy service flourished directly under the eye of the commander-in-chief, usually through one of his aides. Unofficial recognition was given the wives and mistresses of the soldiers. Because they did laundry and cooking and sometimes served as nurses, rations were allowed to them at the rate of three to six per company. They were also permitted to ride in the wagons on long marches. Incredibly, they sometimes packed their children along on campaigns.

The rank and file of the British army were volunteers of a sort. Under the mercantile theory of empire the nation was loath to lose its skilled workers or its farmers from their productive roles in the economy. Consequently, soldiers were drawn from unemployables, vagabonds, adventurers, and jailbirds. They were held under a strict discipline to prevent desertion and were trained to use their weapons. Yet for their time they were as good as any other army in Europe and were probably better treated. The men sometimes turned out to be abler fighters than their officers were commanders, and as a military machine the whole was infinitely superior to the untrained, ill-armed, disputatious aggregation which the Americans put in the field. By all odds the British should have suppressed the Revolution and broken the rebels. How they failed, and why, the succeeding pages endeavor to describe and explain. The war was lost and the war was won, and the complex reasons unfold slowly.

BUNKER HILL

The initiative snatched from him, Gage did nothing for two months. Glumly he heard of a successful rebel raid on May 10, 1775, against dilapidated old Fort Ticonderoga at the southern end of Lake Champlain. A loosely organized band of colonials under rival commanders, Ethan Allen and Benedict Arnold, each commissioned by a different colony, had stormed the place and captured the small garrison—and sixty good cannon.

May passed, and the promised reinforcements did not appear. Half of them arrived in June, the rest in July. Meanwhile, on May 25 the frigate "Cerberus" reached Boston with three major generals: William Howe, John Burgoyne, and Henry Clinton. A London wit characterized this impressive strengthening of Gage's hand with doggerel more truthful than poetic:

> Behold the Cerberus the Atlantic plough,
> Her precious cargo—Burgoyne, Clinton, Howe.
> Bow, wow, wow!

All three were veterans of the Seven Years' War, younger than Gage, and possessing fine military reputations they would now proceed to lose. They found Gage's troops in low spirits. Burgoyne, a member of Parliament and a playwright by avocation, composed a bombastic proclamation for Gage to issue on June

12, imposing martial law and labeling the New England militia and their Whig sympathizers as rebels and traitors; however, pardon was offered to all who would resist and go home. Plans were laid for breaking out of the besieged city. Since eleven hundred reinforcements had now arrived, the generals decided to seize Dorchester Heights, south of the city, on June 18 and begin to roll up the American lines.

Word of this intention was carried to rebel headquarters in Cambridge on June 13. A council of war determined upon fortifying first Bunker Hill, east of Charlestown and north of Boston. In the actual execution of this decision the commanders of the twelve hundred American troops employed decided to dig in on adjacent Breed's Hill because it was closer to Boston. Under cover of darkness, on June 16, they began scooping out a redoubt about forty yards square, throwing up the earth to form a breastwork. As dawn broke on the seventeenth, one of the British warships discovered the intrenchment and boldly opened fire. Her broadside awakened not only the British troops but Gage as well. He forgot about Dorchester Heights as he contemplated this sudden threat.

The British generals met in a council of war. Clinton, who was thirty-seven years old and a good tactician, offered the most sensible suggestion: land troops behind the rebels on Charlestown neck, scale the higher Bunker Hill, and shoot down on the enemy from the rear. Apparently Gage objected to putting a detachment in between two parts of the rebel army. Howe and Burgoyne must have supported him, for the decision was to mount a frontal assault—in the afternoon when the tide was high. Howe would lead four regiments and an artillery company.

Colonel William Prescott, who commanded the Americans,

kept them at their construction work despite the naval bombardment. He was a farmer who revealed himself to be a superb commander in a hot spot. He spread some troops on his left from the redoubt to the water's edge; they had only a stone and rail fence as a cover. On his right Charlestown gave some protection. He sent back for reinforcements, and General Ward reluctantly let him have two regiments. Dr. Warren, now a general, joined Prescott as a volunteer and refused to assume command. Altogether the American force numbered about sixteen hundred men.

Before noon the redcoats began crossing in rowboats, landing east of Breed's Hill. Well out of range, they lunched on their rations and waited. Howe, also a member of Parliament, forty-six years old and inelastic in his military learning, studied the redoubt and sent back for his reserves: another regiment and a battalion of marines under Major Pitcairn of Lexington fame. With the leisurely orthodoxy of the professional, Howe arranged his men and cannon for this set piece and about three o'clock began to move his twenty-two hundred men forward. The elite troops, the light infantry and grenadier companies, plus two regiments, were aimed against the rail fence to turn the American flank and get behind the redoubt. Howe led them. The rest of the force was deployed for a general sweep up the slope of Breed's Hill in the face of the enemy. The ten cannon were to cover this simultaneous advance and roll forward. Back in Boston, people crowded the rooftops in the clear sunshine to watch this rare display of formal attack.

In the crowded redoubt the fatigued diggers awaited the deadly assault. They were told the old cautions: not to fire before ordered, to aim at the crossing of the white belts, to pick out the officers. Prescott was determined upon an effective fire, which must be withheld until it could do maximum damage.

The heavily equipped, even-lined redcoats moved up steadily, over fences and through the grass as if on parade. They fired at intervals by volleys and got no answer. "It is of little purpose to fire at men who are covered with an entrenchment," General James Wolfe had written twenty years earlier, but Howe did not remember. On they came, until Prescott gave the order and the parapet lighted up with stabs of flame. The blast staggered the British; they tried to stand and shoot, but they were hit again and again until they fell back. They had run up against a wall of fire.

Howe himself fared no better. In a column four abreast the light companies marched along the beach toward the rail fence, anxious to avenge Concord. The grenadiers were on their left, a little inland. They caught glimpses through the frail fence of the half-uniformed Americans, strangely quiet and motionless. They were almost near enough to charge, when the fence flamed alive. Those in the lead, privates and officers alike, toppled over. Shouts and cries arose. Other redcoats rushed up and went down under a second fusilade. It was hailing bullets. The columns broke and ran.

Shaken but determined, the British regrouped out of range to try again. The second advance, over dead and wounded comrades, was more harrowing than the first. Again the muskets of the despised enemy mowed them down. Never had the British faced such intense firepower. They faltered. "There was a moment that I never felt before," Howe admitted as he saw his reputation crumbling by a second failure.

Gage, Clinton, and Burgoyne were watching nervously from Boston, hardly able to believe what their glasses revealed. Clinton couldn't stand it. He ordered another regiment and another battalion of marines into boats and crossed ahead of them. On the beach he rallied some retreating soldiers and turned them to face the volcanic hill a third time. Would Howe try again? . . . He had to.

Desperately, Howe shifted his forces more to the left to concentrate on the redoubt and let the men drop their useless packs. Unknown to him, Prescott's deadly fire had used up almost all his men's ammunition. They had left but one or two shots apiece. Prescott sought reinforcements from General Israel Putnam's reserve on Bunker Hill, primarily to get bullets and powder, but the regiments there were mixed together and none too anxious to descend into Prescott's furnace.

The exhausted militia met the third attack with another withering but brief fire. Then their powder was gone. The marines, with bayonets fixed, swarmed over the parapet on three sides, but met a resistance they never forgot. The embattled farmers swung their musket butts and even threw stones. Pitcairn went down to death, but so did Dr. Warren. Prescott, like Howe, led a charmed life and escaped as his men began to flee. Last of all, the men at the rail fence withdrew. A stand was made briefly on Bunker Hill, and then resistance collapsed.

From what he saw, even Burgoyne admitted that "the retreat was no flight; was covered with bravery and even military skill." It was five o'clock, and the British had driven the Americans from the Charlestown peninsula. Howe might have scattered the whole New England army had he pressed on two miles to Cambridge, but he was in no mood to push farther. He had lost over 40 per cent of his detachment, with 226 killed and 828 wounded. "A dear bought victory," Clinton wrote, "another such would have ruined us."

The War for Independence

The American losses were 140 killed, 271 wounded, and only 30 taken prisoner. They did not celebrate, but they were convinced that militia, as long as they had ammunition, could hold off trained regulars, a belief that would give trouble in the future. In truth, they had blundered in occupying so exposed a position and had been saved from annihilation by British stupidity in failing to surround them. Their victory was moral in the account they had given of themselves and, conversely, in the shock they had given Howe and the English people. Even Gage, who had preached against underestimating the colonials, was stung.

These People Shew a Spirit and Conduct against us they never shewed against the French. . . . They are now Spirited up by a Rage and Enthusiasm as great as ever People were possessed of, and you must proceed in earnest or give the Business up. . . . The loss we have Sustained is greater than we can bear.

One further talent the rebels revealed: an awareness of the value of propaganda. Their account of the clash at Lexington and Concord was dispatched promptly to the other colonies and to England before Gage sent his official relation. It was a highly colored narrative that made savages of the redcoats. The Whig opposition applauded the news, and the King's ministry waited impatiently twelve days for a corrective report. But the first impression had been made and was not easily erased. Rumors of the Bunker Hill clash spread in England before Gage's report was published; the official figures told their own grim story. But the stubborn King was made more determined than ever "not [to] be dismayed."

Canada Lost, Carolina Held

Dislodgment of the rebels from Breed's Hill was the second and last offensive step taken by the British army for a year. During the rest of 1775 and through the winter of 1776 they made no effort to break out of the siege that confined them to Boston, partly because they were outnumbered by a militia they grudgingly had to respect and partly because they developed no general plan of action beyond a desire to evacuate the detested city as soon as shipping could be furnished.

Gage was called home in October, 1775, ostensibly to advise the King on requirements for the next campaign, actually to be "let down easy." He was blamed for not having seized the Charlestown heights earlier in the siege and for not having averted the Breed's Hill catastrophe. Burgoyne's frequent letters to London, critical of Gage, also had an effect. The command in North America was then split. Guy Carleton, governor of Canada, was to be chief there, while Howe's authority was to be supreme south of Canada. Handsome and heavy, Howe was indolent, fond of good living and of gambling, and had found a pleasant mistress. Burgoyne, his ambitions disappointed at every turn, sought only to return to London in order to obtain an independent command. Eventually he obtained permission and departed in November. Clinton remained as second to Howe. He talked of striking at New York or one of the southern provinces.

The naval operation was no more effective. Already unequaled on the seas and with a proud tradition of independent action, the British navy co-operated with the army only upon urgent request, and then condescendingly. During the American Revolution it performed miserably under a succession of incompetent admirals, although for the first three years it faced but token opposition from rebel ships. Gage's naval colleague, Admiral Samuel Graves, commanding in American waters, was anything but a fighter. He actually feared the rebels in their whaleboats! He failed to protect the garrison flocks and beeves grazing on the harbor islands. He failed to keep communications open between Boston and other ports. And he failed to attack any ports where the rebels were building privateers. His conduct disgusted the generals and called forth a sarcastic letter from Burgoyne to London, and Graves was replaced in December—by just as procrastinating an admiral, Molyneux Shuldham.

While the British marked time, suffering a serious shortage of food, a lack of fuel, the ravages of smallpox, and complete frustration, the New England rebels were evolving into American belligerents. A Continental army was in the making, its morale as lusty as that of the British was low. Initiative and the offensive rapidly passed across Back Bay to the colonials.

When John Hancock and Sam Adams escaped from Lexington in the April night of 1775, they headed for Philadelphia, where the second Continental Congress, to which they were delegates along with John Adams, would convene on May 10. The session lasted until August 1. The issues before the fifty delegates were complex and unprecedented, but slowly they hammered out a belligerent status and some agreement on ends. In the British Empire the Congress was illegal, of course. Moreover, it had no power over the thirteen colonies represented. The powers of the delegates—who were not unlike ambassadors—were simply to consult and to agree on action if possible. Only a very few representatives spoke of independence; the idea was resisted and even despised. "We have not raised armies with ambitious designs of separating from Great Britain," stated the Congress' "Declaration of Causes of Taking Up Arms." Rhode Island soldiers were enlisted oddly "in His Majesty's service, and in the pay of the Colony of Rhode Island, for the preservation of the Liberties of America."

Whatever political measures might be taken, Congress had either to avow or to disown the militia from several colonies that was besieging Boston. There were both moderates and radicals in Congress, and events from week to week strengthened the stand of the radicals. By the middle of June, Congress approved the proposal by John Adams, an attorney who was beginning to eclipse his rabid cousin Sam, that it "adopt" the army at Boston—that is, supply, regulate, and pay it—and appoint George Washington, forty-three-year-old delegate from Virginia, as its commander-in-chief. It was a superb choice, wiser than even Washington's most enthusiastic admirers could have prophesied. Other men in the colonies were his superiors in intellectual power as well as in military training and battlefield experience, but he could and did learn. What was more important to the cause, no other American possessed his combination of deference to civil authority, fortitude and patience, dignity and bearing. These were the qualities that would carry him through the dark and discouraging days ahead (and thereby support others) and keep the flickering flame of revolution alive. Sensitive to the obligation of a man to live up to his responsibilities, he was strengthened by his great moral integrity. After his appointment he wrote to his wife:

> You may believe me, my dear Patsy, when I assure you, in the most solemn manner that, so far from seeking this appointment, I have used every endeavor in my power to avoid it, not only from my unwillingness to part with you and the family, but from a consciousness of its being a trust too great for my capacity, and that I should enjoy more real happiness in one month with you at home, than I have the most distant prospect of finding abroad, if my stay were to be seven times seven years. But as it has been a kind of destiny that has thrown me upon this service, I shall hope that my undertaking it is designed to answer some good purpose.

A few other generals broke under the tensions, not of the battlefield, but of congressional slowness, indifference of the separate states, uncertain supplies and pay, jealousies of rank, and other irritations that plagued the American military leaders. To Washington these were obstacles to be overcome, not permanent obstructions that justified his resignation. He perceived one factor more clearly than anybody else: the army *was* the Revolution. As long as he could hold an army together, British authority was defied, and a British force had to seek him out to destroy it. Therefore the army must not be dispersed or defeated beyond repair lest the Revolution collapse. And for all his fatigue, harassment, and devotion Washington refused to accept any pay beyond his expenses, which he kept with scrupulous accuracy.

Canada Lost, Carolina Held

Congress also appointed four major generals, none of whom turned out very well: Artemus Ward, who already commanded the Massachusetts troops; Israel Putnam, a vigorous and colorful fifty-seven-year-old Indian fighter from Connecticut; Charles Lee, a brilliant, conceited, and unstable professional officer (he had served in Portugal under Burgoyne) who had retired recently to Virginia and professed to be a great patriot; and Philip Schuyler, another French War veteran and a patrician landowner of northern New York. Horatio Gates, like Lee a former British officer living in Virginia, was named adjutant general. Lee, Schuyler, and Gates set out with Washington for Boston on June 23. Schuyler was left in New York City to command the fortifications ordered to be built there by the Continental Congress.

THE AMERICAN ARMY

On reaching Cambridge and assuming command on July 2, Washington found almost fourteen thousand troops in the vicinity fit for duty. After its initial service at Concord, the militia of New England had been drawn on for men willing to serve until the end of the year 1775. They were variously organized, diversely dressed and equipped, and all in good spirits. Only the Rhode Island troops had tents; the others were quartered in Harvard's dormitories, in private houses, and in soldier-made shelters. Since it was summer, there was a general lack of blankets. Few cannon and almost no trained engineers could be found.

The army lacked uniform appearance for the good reason that it lacked uniforms. The men wore their farming or working clothes and simply added a sword or hung ammunition belts across their shoulders. The long, pullover hunting shirt

25

of linen, woolen, or buckskin eventually was found to be the most practical garb. The common identifying insignia that appeared from time to time was a sprig of laurel worn in the hat. In night marches and attacks it was replaced by a slip of white paper. An occasional regiment was supplied with uniforms, each having its own color combination, and they were the envy of others.

All this "unmilitary" appearance disguised the fighting qualities of the American soldier, the like of which his European and British counterparts had never encountered. Having enjoyed more rights and responsibilities as a citizen, the American displayed more initiative as a soldier—and less discipline. Used to relative equality with his neighbor, he would not be subordinate to him in the army. Hence, officers were elected by the ranks and fraternized freely with the men. As a result discipline hardly existed; courts-martial and punishments were rare; furloughs were frequent. Indeed, the militiaman was essentially a seasonal soldier, an amateur, going home to plant and harvest or ply his trade, and returning to fight.

On the battlefield the American was less the automaton and more the thinking, resourceful antagonist. He had learned from the Indian to take advantage of every natural covert and to fire as an individual with careful aim—and to aim at officers as well as privates. What appeared unfair and cowardly to the European seemed only common sense to the American. Actually the American fought a rougher war. From generations of fighting savages he had learned the futility of showing mercy and giving quarter. The European code of honor was unknown; any means of winning was legitimate, because war was not a game to be won on points but a life-and-death struggle. At the same time, Americans lacked the security of solidarity, of standing shoulder to shoulder with trained comrades. If they would advance as individuals, they would retreat the same way. They did not stay to protect one another. Fear communicated to panic, and withdrawal often degenerated into rout.

Washington's first duty and first great accomplishment was to forge an army out of what he called "this mixed multitude of people." The inactivity of the British gave him the necessary time to whip the men into military competence. He secured supplies, drilled men, weeded out cowardly and lazy officers, detailed his orders each day to educate them, tightened up discipline, built barracks, cleaned up camps and kitchens, soothed regional rivalries, and reported to governors and to Congress. It was all an inglorious, tedious, and exasperating chore. Rifle companies from Pennsylvania, Virginia, and Maryland marched into camp, giving the new army a definitely continental character and jolting the New Englanders by their display of marksmanship and their equipment. Captain Daniel Morgan, whose name is one to remember, marched his company of ninety-six from Virginia in twenty-one days, a distance of six hundred miles, without a man dropping out.

These riflemen were chiefly frontiersmen, and they were equipped with the finest weapon of their day—the Pennsylvania rifle. It had an accuracy which the smoothbore musket could never attain. Rifled barrels were known in Europe, but the problem of making the lead bullet fit snugly, so that it would be set in a whirling motion by the rifle grooves when fired, had been ingeniously solved by some nameless backwoodsman who covered the bullet with a patch of greased linen. Both were inserted in the muzzle and rammed home against a pinch of powder, as in loading the musket. But while the musket was reliable at fifty yards, the rifle was accurate at one hundred and fifty yards. The British sent a captured rifle-man to England as an exhibit, and his demonstration of his weapon had the unexpected effect of discouraging recruiting.

Yet drilling was only half of Washington's job. This army was due to end its term of duty on December 31, 1775. Therefore, in October Washington began recruiting for a Continental army under the authority of Congress to replace it. Officers were to be appointed from the top down rather than elected by the men; enlistments were to run for one year. To achieve uniformity, the forty existing regiments of various sizes had to be reduced to twenty-eight, thus displacing many officers. New regiments were to consist of eight companies, each containing ninety men and officers. All were to furnish their own muskets but would be supplied with clothing and rations and would be paid more than British soldiers. Persons who could bring a blanket would get an extra two dollars.

Despite harangues and entreaties, many of the men refused to enlist in the new Continental army. Congress had refused a bounty, although the provinces had paid one. Washington's regulations were not popular with equality-minded Yankees. Eventually about ten thousand became Continental soldiers—less than half the force Washington was authorized to raise. State militia were called on to supply the remaining half on a temporary basis, but only about seven thousand could be raised.

Attention was also given to the immediate military business at hand: the tightening of the siege of Boston and the launching of any other possible expeditions. Washington improved the fortifications rimming the city and divided the long line of command. Major General Ward, with Brigadiers John Thomas and Joseph Spencer, commanded the southern extension around Roxbury. To the north, Major General Lee, with Brigadiers

Canada Lost, Carolina Held

Nathanael Greene and John Sullivan, took charge. In the center, Cambridge, Major General Putnam was assisted by Brigadier William Heath and a temporary general. Colonel Henry Knox, an erstwhile young Boston bookseller, was learning to manage the insufficient artillery. He was typical of the younger, inexperienced officers who were destined, contrary to reasonable expectation, to emerge as extraordinarily able commanders and to replace some of the first generals who were found lacking.

THE CANADIAN VENTURE

One of the zealous younger officers was Connecticut's Colonel Benedict Arnold, who had shown imagination and dash in the capture of Ticonderoga. He had then run up by boat to seize Fort St. John's on the river outlet of Lake Champlain. Thirty-four years old, powerfully built, he was restless and reckless. His courage was as undeniable as his gnawing egotism was fatal. He had talked of an expedition against Quebec by way of the harsh Maine wilderness. In September Washington decided to use him in such a venture.

Congress had already urged Schuyler to invade Canada in the hope of winning a fourteenth colony to revolt. With unconscionable slowness, he had failed to enlist enough troops until late in August, when his more energetic second-in-command, Brigadier General Richard Montgomery, launched the expedition from Crown Point without him. Schuyler caught up with the detachment outside regarrisoned Fort St. John's, then fell ill and returned south.

While Fort St. John's was under siege, Arnold was leading an intrepid force of more than one thousand volunteers up the Kennebec River in whaleboats. They were to follow the Dead

The War for Independence

River and a chain of ponds to the Height of Land and then to proceed into Lake Megantic and down the Chaudière to the St. Lawrence. It was a grueling, heroic performance of six weeks amid sufferings and setbacks that few commanders would have overcome. The boats, made of green timbers, were both heavy to carry and leaky. The men stumbled over exhausting portages, fought swollen streams and rapids, waded swamps covered with snow, and when provisions gave out even ate their dogs. Arnold had some excellent officers with him: Lieutenant Colonel Christopher Greene of Rhode Island, Major Return Jonathan Meigs of Connecticut, and Captains Dan Morgan of Virginia and Henry Dearborn of New Hampshire—they kept the expedition going. He also had Lieutenant Colonel Roger Enos, who turned back on the Dead River with the rear division of one-fourth of the men and their supplies. This cowardly defection forced Arnold to dash ahead down the Chaudière to get food for his men and send it back. At length, on November 8, seven hundred men, gaunt and worn, reached the St. Lawrence and looked across at formidable Quebec.

Meanwhile, the other rebel force under Montgomery had advanced and taken Montreal on November 13. Governor Guy Carleton, with too small a force to defend the province, escaped to Quebec and found himself in the jaws of a pincer. He had few regular troops in Canada, and if the French there were lukewarm about their liberties, they were just as unenthusiastic about their British government. An aristocrat of fifty-one, Carleton was a nimble and energetic commander who used his meager forces cannily and on whom fortune smiled.

Arnold got his men across the St. Lawrence and moved upstream to effect a juncture with Montgomery's force. Together they could muster only a thousand men fit for duty, but they laid siege to Quebec. Soon they also had winter to combat, then smallpox, then short rations. On December 30, 1775, the day before many of the enlistments ran out, they stormed the walled town at night in a whirling snow. Montgomery was killed, Arnold seriously wounded, and the confused assault dwindled into surrender or escape. The American force was reduced to half its size. Still, from his hospital bed Arnold managed to maintain a siege throughout the winter.

Although Congress sent reinforcements and a new commander, Brigadier General John Thomas, to Montreal in the spring, no further attempt was made against Quebec. On May 4, 1776, Thomas decided to raise the siege. As he departed, three warships brought reinforcements to Carleton. Thomas died of smallpox (a physician, he yet objected to inoculation), and Brigadier General John Sullivan was sent with reinforcements to resolve the situation. He was thirty-five, a New Hampshire lawyer without battle experience, but as an Irishman and a recent delegate to Congress he hated England. This was the first of several forlorn hopes into which he was thrust and from which he could win no glory. He pulled the remnant force back to Montreal and down to Lake Champlain. By the first of July, the northern army was back at Ticonderoga in upstate New York. Canada was irretrievably lost, and the old invasion route into New York was open again.

Though this ambitious and bold undertaking had failed, Washington's pressure on Boston meanwhile had achieved results. Congress would not let him destroy the city, once he had the powder and Colonel Knox had brought some of the captured cannon from Ticonderoga, but he did seize Dorchester Heights and fortified it early in March. Howe knew the game was up, then, for no British ships could remain in the harbor. He decided to move to Halifax, Nova Scotia, to await fresh supplies and reinforcements and to resettle the loyalists who wanted (or were forced) to leave Boston. Word seems to have reached the Americans that the British would not burn the city if they were allowed to leave without being cannonaded or attacked. On March 17, 1776, Howe finished embarking his troops plus about a thousand loyalists and lifted anchor. There was rejoicing in the streets as Washington's troops promptly entered. The American victory was genuine and helped offset the debacle in Canada.

SOUTHERN THRUST

Having failed in New England, British military and cabinet officials searched for another port to seize. Royal governors in the South had begged for military support. Although Massachusetts was the focal point of initial hostilities, it was not the only colony in which revolt flared. Assertive provincial assemblies had forced the governors of North and South Carolina to take refuge aboard British ships. The governor of Georgia was seized as a prisoner, although he later escaped to England. Governor Dunmore of Virginia, having aroused the rebels, was attacked outside loyal Norfolk by Virginia militia. Fleeing aboard a ship, he fired on the town as soon as it was occupied, on New Year's Day, 1776; and the rebels retaliated by burning the town to ashes. Dunmore went home to England.

Governor Martin of North Carolina found means of calling the loyal Scottish highlanders, recently settled in the back country, to rally to his support. A force of more than sixteen hundred marched toward Wilmington, where he waited off-shore. At Moores Creek bridge, eighteen miles north of the town, on February 27, they found eleven hundred rebel militia intrenched under Colonels Richard Caswell and Alexander Lillington. The loyalists attacked and were thrown back violently and quickly, losing more than half their men, mostly as prisoners, as against one rebel killed and one wounded. In addition the victors captured rifles, cannon, wagons, and £15,-000 sterling.

In London the previous November, Lord George Germain (who in Parliament had demanded Gage's recall) had succeeded Lord Dartmouth as Secretary of State for the Colonies. He was an odd choice, not so much because his judgment was inept as because of the well-publicized fact that after the Battle of Minden, 1759, he had been court-martialed for disobedience and cowardice, found guilty, and pronounced unfit ever to serve his Majesty again in any military capacity. That Majesty promptly died, and, as an ardent supporter of George III's ambitions, Germain had licked his way back into favor. He now confidently took charge of suppressing the American rebellion, since he was the only cabinet member with military experience. Contemptuous of the colonial militia, he was entranced by the notion that, with the help and leadership of a few British regulars, the loyalists in the South would rise and overwhelm the hotheaded rebels. He therefore agreed to send reinforcements directly from England under Lord Charles Cornwallis and Vice-Admiral Sir Peter Parker. They would join a detachment from Howe under General Clinton off the mouth of Cape Fear River in North Carolina.

Winter storms and other delays held up Cornwallis' departure until April, about the time that Clinton reached the Cape

Fear River from Boston. When Clinton learned of the action at Moores Creek bridge and in Norfolk, he realized that the time to inspire an uprising of loyalists had passed; hardly one now dared open his mouth. Yet he felt obliged to do something. When Cornwallis and Parker finally hove in sight in May, he had decided to surprise Charleston by a combined naval and army attack. The city of twelve thousand was the largest in the South.

What he did not know was that Congress had considered Charleston a possible point of attack for five months and accordingly had added twelve southern battalions to the Continental army and ordered Charles Lee to command them. South Carolina had called out her militia and encouraged Colonel William Moultrie to erect fortifications, principally on Sullivan's Island, one of several at the harbor entrance. Moultrie built a fort with double walls of palmetto logs sixteen feet apart and filled between with earth, and with four bastions for thirty cannon. Fort Johnson on James Island guarded the south side of the harbor. Batteries were set up at other points so that an aggregate of about a hundred guns pointed seaward. More than six thousand troops were distributed in the vicinity when Admiral Parker sailed his squadron into this hornet's nest on June 1, 1776.

The surprise lost, everything went wrong with the attack. Clinton's troops were not landed until June 9, on Long Island, just outside the harbor. They were to cross a ford eighteen inches deep at low tide to Sullivan's Island, after the warships had shelled the frail-looking fort. When someone measured the depth of the water at the ford, Clinton discovered to his "unspeakable mortification" that the water was seven feet deep! His army now was truly *hors de combat*. He began a rapid correspondence with the admiral, declaring what he would do under certain circumstances if the navy covered him. Parker grew confused but, foreseeing an independent naval victory anyway, proceeded with his own plans to reduce the fort. The Americans threw up two batteries on the north point close to Long Island and discouraged Clinton further. Co-operation between the British services, rarely good, reverted to its normal chilly distance.

Contrary winds held up the naval attack until June 28, when Parker sent three frigates through a narrow passage to cover the west side of Fort Sullivan. They ran aground, and one was abandoned and burned. These were the vessels Clinton counted on to cover his crossing to the mainland. Six ships were to blast the fort from the east. Two of them carried fifty guns each, the others twenty-two to twenty-eight, so that the British had five guns for each one fired by Moultrie. Action began at eleven o'clock in the morning of a hot day with the heaviest shelling the veteran Lee had ever heard or seen. Gradually Parker realized that the miserable fort was taking all the balls his cannon could deliver without any sign of destruction. This was his first experience with palmetto, a spongy wood which absorbed the cannon balls as if swallowing them. The thick dirt walls held. The well-protected rebels returned the shelling with deadly fire. The bombardment duel stretched out for ten hours. Lee, who had rested little faith in the fort and had predicted it would fall in half an hour, was amazed by the courage and endurance of Moultrie's 380 men. The proud British ships were severely damaged, and British casualties mounted to 225 dead and wounded. Parker's flagship suffered most, and the admiral experienced the climactic indignity of having his breeches blown off. At nine o'clock in the evening he called it quits. The land commanders, Clinton and Lee, had been able to do little more than watch. The South was safe for two years, and Charleston for four.

With this British failure in mid-1776, the first year of the war ended. There had been no strategy on either side. Hostilities had flamed from a little flash in the pan at Lexington. Thereafter each side traded blows as opportunities arose. Although the rebels had failed to win Canada, they had pushed the British out of New England and had blocked their invasion of the South. With an army in the field and a year of congressional experience in directing a war, the Americans had definitely come off the better of the two, but Washington was well aware that the British lion had been shaken awake and was getting to its feet. A big offensive was in the making, and most likely it was pointed at New York.

Colonial morale was high. People were discussing a political question: Was there, after all, any difference between the "good King" to whom they professed loyalty and the "bad ministry" which had sent troops against them? Was not the ministry composed of the King's friends, whose advice he readily sought when they were not following his? A popular pamphlet called *Common Sense*, written by a recent English emigrant, Thomas Paine, had been published at Philadelphia late in January, 1776. It offered a hard-hitting argument that the colonies were foolish to respect the King and could obtain their avowed ends only by independence, never by reconciliation. Indeed, the logical extension of the constitutional argument the colonies had been building since resisting taxation in 1765 called either for equality within a commonwealth of British nations (a concept truly revolutionary to imperialism) or for an independent new nation.

Canada Lost, Carolina Held

On July 4, 1776, Congress voted its decision for a people made ready for it during the past year. They were finally convinced that the rights they prized and the self-government they desired could be secured only by sovereign status. With the solemn Declaration of Independence, the rebels were now legal belligerents and might properly be termed "Americans." They were fighting *for* something now, as well as against something.

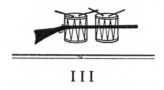

I I I

To the Delaware—and Back

Convinced at last that the American revolt might become a major war, Parliament determined to bring it to a speedy end by providing the massive force that Gage had advised at the outset. An army of fifty-five thousand was authorized for America, but recruiting proceeded so slowly that several German princes were appealed to for mercenaries. English subsidies to European armies were nothing new, and these princes were relatives or friends of George III's Hanoverian family. Altogether thirty thousand German troops were hired at varying fees paid to their rulers, seventeen thousand of them from Hesse-Cessel. In consequence, all of them were dubbed "Hessians" in America, a term spit out in contempt. British and German troops destined for America in 1776 amounted to forty-two thousand, an ample number if properly deployed and led. Yet this powerful blade was not to be wielded lustily.

In England the American Revolution was a political issue. The King and his friends, chiefly Tories, had sought to ease the financial burden left by the Seven Years' War by getting money from the colonies. For a dozen years they had tried various tax measures without success and produced only revolt. The parliamentary minority, largely Whig, had supported many of the American protests and arguments as opposition policy. Their aim was not to deny the supremacy of Parliament over the colonies but to embarrass and reduce the political power of the King. If George III wished to continue exercising the power he loved, then he must defeat the American colonies. First, he had to do it promptly, before his old enemies, France and Spain, should be tempted to make matters worse for him. Second, he must do it cheaply. War cost money and added to the national debt, while armed occupation of defeated colonies would require more funds than could be extracted from them by taxation. Therefore the object of victory was not bitterness, which would ruin the King too, but colonial reconciliation to the idea of sharing the cost of empire. It was to be a limited war.

Concentrating on the army rather than the navy as the primary instrument of victory, Britain decided to divide the colonies and expose the weakness of the separated regions. The commanders were empowered to accept submission before launching their invasion; if that failed, they were to give battle, demonstrate their military superiority, then offer an armistice again at some favorable moment. Even the stubborn Americans would soon see the foolishness of persisting in their own ruination when it was so unnecessary.

The strategic plan called for securing first of all a better base than Boston. New York City was selected because of both its splendid harbor and its location at the mouth of a waterway that divided the colonies. General Howe would descend from Halifax and, after being heavily reinforced, would occupy the

American city of twenty-five thousand. Then he would extend a line north to control the Hudson, while a Canadian expedition under Carleton would push the Americans off Lake Champlain and reach Albany. New England might be invaded from the west if necessary. Naval power under Admiral Richard Howe, the general's able brother, could be expected to cooperate smoothly with the military in dominating the Hudson. It also could destroy any seaport, or make it a base of naval supplies, and enforce a general blockade.

The Howe brothers, who actually were Whigs, therefore carried with them a commission to make peace as soon as their show of tremendous force induced the Americans to consider reconciliation. Unfortunately for such an initial hope, they did not reach New York Harbor until after the Declaration of Independence had been adopted and an enthusiastic mob in the city had pulled down an equestrian lead statue of George III to be melted into bullets. Nevertheless, the brothers tried to arrange a conference with Washington, but stupidly addressed the American commander-in-chief as "Mr. Washington" or "George Washington, Esq.," and the latter quite correctly refused to receive their letters. Their adjutant was told that the commissioners would have to negotiate with Congress anyway, whereupon the Howes gave over their halfhearted effort and turned to planning their attack on the city. Their subsequent military efforts seemed equally halfhearted, as if they continued to expect signs of an armistice.

A chastened Clinton returned from his Charleston failure on August 1, 1776, with Parker's battered squadron. The main contingent of reinforcements from Europe, with camp equipage, arrived on the twelfth. The Howes now had thirty-two thousand troops, ten thousand seamen, four hundred transports, and thirty fighting ships. Never had the New World seen such a formidable concentration of military strength; it surpassed the armada that had besieged Louisbourg in 1758 or taken Quebec in 1759. But summer was waning. Finally, on August 22, twenty thousand British and Hessian troops were landed on the Gravesend beaches of Long Island to attack the American lines in front of fortified Brooklyn. Heavily booted and equipped, the Hessians were something of a sight, with most of them mustached and all of them wearing long greased queues.

THE LOSS OF NEW YORK

Foreseeing the blow at New York, Washington had sent Lee to plan the defense of the city, but Lee could do little before Congress ordered him south to save Charleston. Leaving Ward to command the Boston area, Washington himself had taken most of the Continental army to New York in the spring. Congress ordered militia support from New York and from her neighbors to the south. Manhattan Island was not easy to defend. Aside from the small forts and redoubts under construction by Lee's order, Fort Washington and Fort Lee were built to guard the Hudson, gun batteries were placed in the Lower Bay, some streets were barricaded, old hulks were sunk in channels, and even a giant chain was forged to be stretched across the Hudson at Fort Montgomery, near West Point. However, shipping could still move up both sides of Manhattan Island. Intrenchments protected Brooklyn, for the heights there commanded New York City and had to be held.

Washington had to scatter his army in five divisions: one on northern Manhattan under Heath; three in the city under Putnam, Spencer, and Sullivan, who had come back from the northern retreat; and the fifth on Long Island under Nathanael Greene. The latter general went down with malaria in August, and Sullivan was shifted to the more exposed command. After the British landed, Washington moved Putnam's division over to Brooklyn, and as ranking major general Putnam took command of the eight to nine thousand troops. Personally brave and vigorous, he was no tactician and was unable to handle so many men. He stationed half his troops outside the town to the south under Sullivan and Brigadier General William Alexander, Lord Stirling, a hard-drinking, New Jersey officer who claimed a lapsed Scottish earldom.

With a preponderant force and shrewd tactics, Howe launched on the night of August 26 a double-pronged attack. While Major General James Grant and the Hessians engaged Sullivan and Stirling in a frontal assault, Clinton and Cornwallis were dispatched in a wide arc east and north around to the American rear. By dawn Sullivan was hotly committed but holding. Fighting was violent in spots, and the Hessians earned a bestial reputation for slaughtering the Americans who had surrendered. Then Sullivan heard firing behind him as Clinton completed his encirclement. Panicked, the Americans turned and began running for the intrenchments of Brooklyn. Still fighting and furious, luckless Sullivan was captured in a cornfield. On his right Stirling had held back Grant's five thousand British with his seventeen hundred men (mostly from Delaware and Maryland). But after Sullivan's defeat, the Hessians swung against his flank and Cornwallis rushed across to block his retreat. Stirling, too, gave up. It was a stinging but honorable defeat for the Americans. They had lost fourteen hundred in killed, wounded, and captured, as against the enemy's loss of less than four hundred.

To the Delaware—and Back

Howe might have overrun Brooklyn and captured the forces there, but, cautious and indolent, he halted his men in the afternoon and on the next day began intrenchments and earthworks for a siege operation, hampered by rain. Washington, who had crossed to Brooklyn during the battle, held a council of war on the twenty-ninth and was advised to evacuate. With his back to open water and outnumbered, he was in grave danger of being cut off. Before he left New York, he had ordered Heath to gather into the East River all the boats he could find. They were ordered down at dusk, and Colonel John Glover's regiment of Massachusetts fishermen began their extraordinary task of transporting the troops to the lower end of Manhattan Island in a rainstorm. The operation was conducted so quietly that the enemy never knew what was happening, and the Americans brought off all their guns, horses, ammunition, and food. No British ships interfered. By the time a foggy dawn cleared, Washington himself stepped into one of the last boats. Brooklyn was empty, as the chagrined Howe shortly discovered. Nevertheless, he was knighted for this victory.

Masterly as the withdrawal was, it could not offset a defeat that opened New York to easy invasion. Greene boldly suggested burning the city, but Congress had ordered Washington not to harm it. The militia was deserting in droves after experiencing battle. Washington established a new line along the Harlem River but left Putnam's division in the city for political reasons. For two weeks Howe delayed, offering the olive branch again by dispatching the captured Sullivan to Congress with proposals for peace. Benjamin Franklin, John Adams, and young Edward Rutledge were appointed to meet Admiral Howe at Staten Island. The delegation demanded recognition of independence as the first condition of negotiation. Howe revealed that he had no real power to negotiate, only to accept submission and stop the fighting. The impasse was complete.

Hostilities resumed on September 15, when General Howe sent a force under Clinton to land part way up Manhattan Island on the east side. It was to strike across the island and seal off Putnam's division. Washington advanced to head off the invasion and held open a corridor along the west side until Putnam got his men safely northward. From Harlem Heights next day Washington sent a British advance reeling and inflicted twice as many casualties as he received. The engagement did much to restore morale among the Americans. Nevertheless, Howe occupied the city and dawdled there, his victory marred by a mysterious fire that burned one-fourth of the city and made billets more cramped for his troops.

At length, in mid-October, 1776, Howe set out again to take advantage of the rivers and move around behind Washington. Putting his men in boats, he sailed close to New Rochelle and landed at Pell's Point. Colonel Glover had posted there four Massachusetts regiments that resisted the four thousand enemy with surprising effectiveness on October 18. Protected behind stone walls lining the only road inland and having three cannon, the Americans delivered a terrific wallop. Even yet the enemy casualties are a mystery. Howe reported three killed and twenty-two wounded, but these were British only and obviously too few for an engagement that lasted all day. Three-fourths of his force was made up of Germans, and if they suffered in proportion, casualties must have amounted to a hundred. British deserters in the next few days estimated their loss at from one hundred fifty to one thousand! Certain at least is the fact that the jolt stopped Howe for three days, until he obtained reinforcements.

To the Delaware—and Back

Washington had withdrawn northward ahead of the enemy and established a camp at a strong position near White Plains. Sullivan and Stirling had rejoined him after an exchange of prisoners. However, he had left behind under Greene two thousand men in Fort Washington and thirty-five hundred in Fort Lee, opposite each other on the Hudson. Howe attacked Washington on October 28, seized a hill on the left, then waited three days for more reinforcements newly arrived from Europe. Just as he was ready to launch his power drive, Washington pulled back five miles to North Castle.

Deflated, Howe moved west and south to the Hudson at Dobbs Ferry. Although he had failed to bring Washington to a decisive battle or to get behind him, he now was in a position to overrun Fort Washington. To hold on or to evacuate was left to Nathanael Greene's decision, and he wrongly believed that Colonel Robert Magaw could defend the fort. To strengthen it, he gave Magaw an additional nine hundred men. Washington sent Heath to Peekskill with three thousand men, left Lee at North Castle with fify-five hundred, and took the remaining two thousand into New Jersey and joined Greene at Fort Lee. They recrossed the river to inspect Fort Washington on November 16, the day Howe opened his attack. They saw the defense crumble under overpowering odds and stayed until a few minutes before Magaw had to surrender. The fight lasted two hours, and the American garrison inflicted 452 casualties, three times as many as it suffered. But Washington had lost twenty-nine hundred troops.

Two days later Cornwallis crossed the Hudson and struck at Fort Lee. Greene narrowly escaped with his garrison, losing his tents, cannons, ammunition, and a hundred skulkers. As a general he was still learning. At thirty-four he was the youngest of the first crop of brigadiers. By trade an anchorsmith, he had been a Quaker until read out of meeting. He limped from a knee injury and suffered from asthma; yet he developed into Washington's ablest general.

For two and a half months Washington had been fighting defensively, sparring, withdrawing, trying to hold his weary army together. Now in November, 1776, began his darkest month of retreat and agonizing disintegration. Howe pressed him laggardly but persistently, and he fell back southwestward across New Jersey toward Philadelphia. Flour, tents, blankets, and intrenching tools had been lost in great quantity in the two forts. Desertions raveled the edges of his dispirited army. The New Jersey militia failed to muster for reinforcements; indeed, the state government broke up and fled. He called for Lee to bring the troops from North Castle, but that overly ambitious sloven dallied in conceited hope of succeeding the commander-in-chief. Washington backed down the road to Trenton, depressed further by learning that Clinton had sailed against Rhode Island. Sweeping up all the river boats he could find, Washington fled across the Delaware into Pennsylvania on December 7, twenty-four days before the enlistments of his Continentals would expire. It began to snow.

In the process of overrunning New Jersey with such ease, Howe aroused more bitter hatred and created more staunch rebels than his proffer of pardons won to the King. His troops demonstrated to innocent Americans what military invasion meant in European style. Residents may have expected to lose their horses and livestock to the enemy, but the pillaging advanced to the robbery of food, silver plate, jewelry, bric-a-brac, and blankets. Officers helped themselves to wine, books, and furniture. The camp followers, like harpies, even stole clothing for themselves and their children. The Germans utilized carts to carry off quantities of articles they never could use. Rape was practiced, too. A rebel's complaint that "These damn'd Invaders play the very devil with the Girls and even old Women. . . . There is Scarcely a Virgin to be found in the part of the Country they have pass'd thro!" may be discounted as exaggeration for propaganda. But what is to be thought of the insolent Lord Francis Rawdon's comment?

> The fair nymphs of this isle [Staten Island] were in wonderful tribulation, as the fresh meat our men have got here has made them riotous as satyrs. A girl cannot step into the bushes to pluck a rose without running the most imminent risk of being ravished, and they are so little accustomed to these vigorous methods they don't bear them with the proper resignation, and of consequence we have most entertaining court-martials every day.

As for the Germans, courts-martial for such acts did not occur to them.

Washington also complained of the treatment of American prisoners of war. The King had proclaimed the rebels to be traitors, and the ministry wanted to treat them as criminals deserving death. The British military in America disagreed from necessity, since the Americans had too many prisoners on whom to retaliate. Nevertheless, prisoners of the British received scandalous care and died in confinement, often in the foul holds of prison ships, while others emerged unfit to serve as soldiers again. Washington accused Howe directly of promoting such cruelty so as to exchange for a healthy British soldier an emaciated American who could only be discharged.

LAKE CHAMPLAIN

Far to the north a forlorn hope had unaccountably revived. A British thrust that should have penetrated to Albany was parried and the blade broken. Carleton had been reinforced in the late spring with regulars and Hessians under General Burgoyne. Adding some Canadians and Indians, he had a force of nearly ten thousand gathered at Fort St. John's, where a small fleet was under construction to carry the invaders to the south end of Lake Champlain. This expedition was a renewal of the drive against Arnold, but now co-ordinated with Howe's assault on New York City.

Carleton did not intend to leave approximately three thousand Americans to convalesce and re-equip in Fort Ticonderoga; they were off balance, and he intended to press his advantage. To embark his army, however, was a prodigious task. Three ships from England were knocked to pieces at Montreal, carried overland to St. John's, and put together again. Twenty gunboats, one floating battery, and two hundred flat-bottomed barges for transport were constructed for the invasion. Carleton's summer of opportunity waned, and September colored the lake shores before he was ready.

Meanwhile, Arnold had recovered from his leg wound and was as busy and indomitable as ever. He had no intention of waiting to be bagged. Schuyler, who still commanded the Northern Department, kept his headquarters at Albany and sought to raise militia to throw against the coming red tide. To assist him, Congress assigned Major General Gates to the north. While the two of them recruited, they let Arnold pursue his mad, impossible plan. He was going to build an American fleet and sail against Carleton!

Shipwrights and sawyers, sailcloth and naval supplies were requisitioned from New England. Axmen felled trees on the lake shore, and green timbers were hewn into ships—two schooners, two sloops, four galleys, and eight gondolas. Cannon were mounted on the unpainted decks, and the unseaworthy craft were manned by soldiers. Despite the handicaps of supplies and haste, Arnold was ready the first week in October—a few days ahead of Carleton.

Boldly Arnold sailed north past abandoned Crown Point to Valcour Island, three-quarters of the way down the lake. There he placed his flotilla in battle line between the western shore and the island to wait. Carleton's squadron confidently approached this minor barrier on October 11. The British ships were better built and better gunned, and they were manned by Royal Navy tars and officers. Sailing down the east side of the island, they tacked around it and faced Arnold from the south, intent on wiping out this arrogant advance.

Yet for seven hours the desperate Americans fought them to a standstill. Once a West India trader, Arnold displayed unorthodox skill in handling his ships, and the gunners gave as good as they received. On shore Indians joined the battle by climbing trees and firing down on the decks of the American ships. By sunset Carleton had to disengage in order to refit, but he established a line to prevent the escape of his enemy. Since Arnold had lost a schooner and gondola plus many of his men, Carleton was sure he could capture the battered fleet next morning. In a fog Arnold slipped through the line with his unseemly ships and headed south. The British pursued him, of course, and caught up on the second day. Another fateful battle followed. The Americans slugged it out in a running fight until their ships caught fire or began to go down under them. When his own galley was put out of action, Arnold signaled the remaining vessels to run aground. The surviving troops clambered off, set fire to their gallant craft, and escaped through the woods to Crown Point and thence back to Ticonderoga. They had fought a magnificent delaying action of greater import than they could imagine.

Carleton was not quite unnerved. He landed his troops and occupied Crown Point. At his leisure, he scouted Ticonderoga but apparently had no stomach for beginning a siege so late in the season. Suddenly on November 4, for reasons not clear even now, he embarked his troops and returned to St. John's and Montreal. Burgoyne, having expected to win new laurels with this expedition, was furious. The invasion threat from the north vanished for the winter. General Schuyler released Gates to reinforce the retreating Washington. Arnold was dispatched to Rhode Island, where the British were threatening Newport.

THE NINE DAYS' WONDER

Holding a thin line on the Delaware River, Washington desperately needed all the men he could get. If the British were not building boats for crossing the river in force, it was because they knew they didn't have to. In a few more days the river would freeze, and they could walk across. This development probably would coincide with the expiration of the enlistment of his veterans. In other words, Washington could lose by inaction as easily as he could by risking an action.

Congress indicated its expectations by removing from Philadelphia to Baltimore. Lee had gotten under way at last, only to get himself captured at a tavern outside Basking Ridge—apart from his troops. Washington as much as Congress lamented this loss, although Lee's subsequent behavior would suggest that a more favorable piece of luck could hardly have happened. Washington's gloom reached its nadir on December 18, when he unburdened himself to his brother John in a confidential letter:

To the Delaware—and Back

I think the game is pretty near up. . . . You can form no Idea of the perplexity of my Situation. No Man, I believe, ever had a greater choice of difficulties and less means to extricate himself from them.

Two days later he was feeling more confident. Sullivan brought in Lee's division, which had shrunk to two thousand by desertions and expired enlistments, and Gates arrived with six hundred men. Pennsylvania militia turned out to the number of two thousand, now that the war had reached their own state. Altogether Washington's strength totaled seventy-six hundred. Then Tom Paine, the *Common Sense* author who had attached himself to Greene's staff as a volunteer during the retreat, turned out an eloquent essay called "The American Crisis." It appeared in the Philadelphia *Journal,* and Washington order it read before each regiment. It began:

These are the times that try men's souls. The summer soldier and the sunshine patriot will, in this crisis, shrink from the service of his country; but he that stands it Now, deserves the love and thanks of man and woman. Tyranny, like hell, is not easily conquered; yet we have this consolation with us, that the harder the conflict, the more glorious the triumph.

Washington began to meditate on a counterattack before his time ran out. He looked across at Trenton and below at Bordentown. They were garrisoned by Hessians, about twenty-five hundred strong. A sudden swoop. . . . The problem was the river. He called in Colonel Glover, the short, reliable redhead. Washington probably got his answer in one word from the reticent fisherman.

Howe had actually given up the pursuit of Washington and gone into winter quarters. It appeared to him that rebel resistance was disintegrating, that by holding Rhode Island and New York he could take Philadelphia in the spring, then move southward to stamp out any remaining hostility. He had re-

51

turned to New York, given Cornwallis leave to go home to England, and at the end of his overextended line running southwestward from New York had placed his Hessian allies in garrison at Trenton and Bordentown under Colonels Johann Rall and Christian von Donop.

Washington called a council of war and outlined a surprise attack. He himself would take twenty-four hundred Continentals, cross the river, and descend on Trenton from the north. General James Ewing was to take a few hundred of his Pennsylvania militia across just below Trenton and cut off the road to Bordentown. Colonel John Cadwalader was to have eighteen hundred men, half Continentals and half militia, to move on Bordentown itself. Washington asked for three days' provisions to be cooked and the boats he had seized in his retreat three weeks before to be brought down in the darkness. The date for crossing: Christmas night, 1776.

"Granny" Gates suddenly found urgent business with Congress, but Greene, Sullivan, Knox, and the others were all for it. Glover's men brought down the Durham boats—oversized canoes forty feet long, eight feet wide, pointed at both ends, and operated by sails and poles. Christmas night ushered in probably the worst weather of the month, with falling temperature, a high wind, and blocks of ice riding the current. Knox had charge of loading the troops and cannon, as only his booming voice could carry against the wind. He was twenty-six years old, already plump and jovial, and had all the appearance of a fireside, armchair general. The surprising thing about him was his consistent activity: he was all of a piece, no more perturbed in a nocturnal blizzard on the Delaware River than he would have been in a warm tavern after closing his bookshop. Well-nigh indestructible, he became an exceptionally competent artillerist and eventually Secretary of War.

The crossing was made at McKonkey's Ferry, the slow, cold job lasting until three o'clock in the morning. Then there were nine miles to march. Halfway to Trenton the column paused to eat and then divided. Sullivan took half the men and cannon and held to the road close to the river. Greene took the remainder to the left so as to approach the town from the northeast. Near dawn, snow began to fall, then changed to sleet and glazed the rutted roads. The weary, half-frozen men slipped and slid; the cannon were almost uncontrollable.

Challenged in the murky dawn by a Hessian patrol, Greene's men rushed on to the head of two parallel Trenton streets that met their road at right angles. Musket shots from Sullivan's division behind the town indicated his arrival. Knox rolled up his cannon and began raking the streets as if he were bowling. The Hessians had been slow in rousing after a festive Christmas night and now could not form ranks in the streets. Colonel Rall ordered his men into the open fields. They formed once and tried to charge into town, but it was already overrun by the Americans from two directions. When Rall himself was shot down, the demoralized troops thought only of escape or surrender. About two hundred fled toward Bordentown (Ewing had failed to cross), but more than nine hundred gave up. When Washington asked for his own casualties, he found four men slightly wounded! With no word from Cadwalader and a big bag of prisoners on his hands, Washington reluctantly concluded not to press his luck by pushing on to Princeton. He ordered a withdrawal across the river.

Cadwalader, who had been unable to get his men across the

river to attack Bordentown, persisted and made the leap on the twenty-seventh. The Hessians there did not wait to dispute him, but fled up to Princeton, to which place Cornwallis was hurriedly ordered to retrieve the loss. When Washington heard of Cadwalader's success, he ordered fresh rations and prepared to invade New Jersey again. On December 30 he took his men into Trenton and waited for Cadwalader to join him. At the same time Washington began a program of addressing each regiment of veterans, urging them to re-enlist even for just six weeks, offering a bounty of ten dollars, and promising better care and more glorious opportunities. It was heartbreaking work, but his earnestness was persuasive. Sometimes he won less than half a regiment; again, almost all. He sent General Thomas Mifflin, an eloquent speaker, to harangue Cadwalader's Continental brigade. Late in the day they had won over two-thirds to three-fourths of the men. The sick, the weaklings, and the self-centered were gone, although some would re-enlist later.

Congress had actually authorized an army of eighty-eight "battalions" (i.e., regiments) to be raised, and another sixteen regiments for duty in the South. Altogether this establishment envisioned seventy thousand men under arms, plus three regiments of artillery and four of dragoons. Only half that number was ever recruited, and but part of them turned up for duty.

On New Year's Day, 1777, Cadwalader's troops joined Washington, and he laid out a line behind a creek on the south edge of Trenton. There were those who wondered if he knew what he was about, waiting for the British to storm down on him from Princeton. Leading the enemy force was a disgruntled Lord Cornwallis, yanked back from his leave, A tall, portly aristocrat, he had suffered a head injury in youth that gave a cast to one eye. He found himself forced to spar with an American brigade that delayed his entrance to Trenton until dusk of January 2. He was sure he could capture the American camp in the morning.

But behind his brightly burning campfires, Washington peeled off his men noiselessly and marched them eastward around the enemy. By morning they were in sight of Princeton. When Cornwallis bestirred himself in Trenton he looked out on some smoldering campfires, a few piles of dirt, and a lifeless landscape. He swore to himself.

Two British regiments on their way out of Princeton to support Cornwallis were startled to see the enemy approaching in force on their left. General Hugh Mercer took 350 Virginians into an orchard to meet them. The two detachments exchanged volleys; then some of the Virginians came running back, frightening the militiamen who were coming up. Perceiving the start of a rout, Washington spurred his horse forward, called for the men to form, and personally led a charge into the face of the enemy. A magnificent horseman, he became an irresistible leader. The men followed him to within thirty yards of the redcoats before he gave the order to fire. The terrific volley enveloped him in smoke. When it cleared he was still sitting calmly on his horse. The militia and Continentals cheered; the British fell back and once in motion had the Americans after them. Washington stood up in his stirrups and waved.

"It's a fine fox chase, my boys!"

The British were routed. Some of them sought refuge in Princeton, but Washington's van soon penetrated the college town and captured those who had not fled beyond. The Americans found precious blankets, shoes, and flour. They ate and rested two hours before the outraged Cornwallis, smarting under his deception, had turned his army around and hurried up the Post Road—only to be stopped by a demolished bridge. He then had but one goal: to get to Brunswick, the big supply depot of the British that housed a pay chest of £70,000 in gold. Washington knew about the military chest, too, and had been sorely tempted to beat him to it, but his men had marched all night and some of them had fought. He took them northward into the hills around Morristown and there made winter quarters.

Washington had engineered an astonishing reversal of fortune. The long British line that threatened Philadelphia had been rolled up to Brunswick. Howe and Cornwallis had lost prestige here and in London. Congress was elated, the captured Hessians were paraded through Philadelphia, and New Jersey was no longer neutral. The gloomy American states were electrified. Most of all, Washington's faith had been justified, his hope restored. The Revolution was not going to collapse.

Promotions to brigadier general were awarded Colonels Glover, Knox, and Cadwalader. Mercer had died of multiple wounds.

British strategy had succeeded in part yet had missed its goal. New York City had been captured, but the victory was without decisive effect in subduing the colonists. Carleton had failed in the North, and Howe had neglected to destroy Washington's army. Little use had been made of sea power except to support the army. Peace overtures had never gotten off the ground. The British effort that had seemed so mighty at the start of the campaign had somehow dissipated itself like a blown-out tornado.

In England, that noted gossip Horace Walpole grudgingly wrote of Washington: "His march through our lines is allowed to have been a prodigy of generalship."

In his Potsdam palace, Frederick the Great was gleeful over the defeat of the Hessians he despised. As he pored over maps to follow Washington's ensuing move, he reputedly called it the most brilliant campaign of the century.

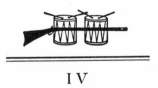

I V

"A Thousand Untoward Circumstances"

The British campaign of 1777 was to complete and extend the strategy envisioned the year before. Of course, it was to be the final campaign.

The fabric was tailored in London by that incompetent apprentice, Lord Germain. His first pattern was drawn by General Howe, who roused himself sufficiently to propose marching ten thousand men into Pennsylvania to seize the rebel capital, rout the Congress, and arm the loyalists. He would leave two thousand men in garrison at Newport, Rhode Island, four thousand in New York City, and three thousand on the lower Hudson, partly to "facilitate in some degree the approach of the army from Canada," which Howe expected to reach Albany in September. The total of nineteen thousand troops committed did not include the loyalists in arms (whom the British called provincials). Germain indorsed this plan, although what was to be gained by seizing Philadelphia if Washington's army remained intact defied answer, as the inconclusiveness of capturing New York had already demonstrated.

A different cut to the garment was advocated by Burgoyne, who returned to England again at the end of 1776. He proposed to succeed where Carleton had failed by a descent from Canada over two routes: via Lake Champlain, and from the west via Lake Ontario and the Mohawk River; the two routes were to converge on Albany. On reaching that town he would arrange with Howe for the control of the Hudson River so as to cut off New England and to enable Howe "to act with his whole force to the southward." Germain liked this pattern, too, and the three thousand men Howe was leaving for cooperative use seemed ample. Burgoyne, of course, was named to command the northern army; Carleton, whom Germain disliked, was knighted and left to his civil duties as governor. Howe was informed of Burgoyne's plan.

The fundamental weakness of Burgoyne's scheme, however, was the same as Howe's: its success would not end the war. Cutting the communication between New England and the other colonies was not fatal; New England would not be taken out of the war unless its coast were blockaded too, and only then after a long passage of time.

Just as Germain began to sew up his cloth, he received a revised pattern from Howe. On counting his men again, the general had decided to leave twenty-four hundred at Newport, forty-seven hundred in New York plus three thousand provincials to serve defensively around the city, and to take eleven thousand to Philadelphia *by sea*. Germain should have gulped at this realignment, for the three thousand regulars who were to push up the Hudson at Burgoyne's call were not in the picture. Howe cannot be excused for this omission merely because he wrote to Carleton that neither he nor Burgoyne should count on aid from him. Moreover, in approaching Philadelphia by water Howe would establish no overland communication with New York. Why he made these new decisions never has been determined. As for Germain, he may have thought the very fact that Howe would keep Washington engaged in Pennsylvania would serve Burgoyne adequately by clearing his path. So he approved this altered plan, too, expressing only the hope that Howe would be victorious in time to assist Burgoyne up the Hudson. Having committed himself to a strategy of double envelopment, Germain was responsible for co-ordinating the two expeditions so as to avoid simultaneous commitment in two widely separated theaters.

Germain, the King, Howe, Burgoyne—all of them may be excused for failing to anticipate one fatal development: no one could have believed then that a *second* American army, *larger* than Washington's, would be raised in the vicinity of Albany and thrown against Burgoyne. But none of them is to be forgiven for making plans to end the war that overlooked the absolute necessity of drawing Washington into battle and destroying his army.

BURGOYNE'S INVASION

About four thousand British and three thousand German troops were assembled in Canada in June, 1777, for Burgoyne's trek, a total of seven thousand or more, plus, it is reported, two thousand women! He had able subordinates in Major General William Phillips, a veteran artilleryman, in Brigadier General Simon Fraser, and in Major General Baron Friedrich Adolph von Riedesel of Brunswick, a warmhearted cavalryman, thirty-nine years old, whose wife and children traveled the wilderness with him. Carleton assisted by calling in militia and Indians, but neither group responded with any enthusiasm after the past year's experience. Only about two hundred and fifty French-Canadians and American loyalists enrolled, and some fourteen hundred Indians showed up for the bloodletting. Commanding one band of warriors was Governor Carleton's nephew Christopher, a man with an Indian as well as a white wife, who dressed like a savage, painted his face, and wore a ring in his nose.

Burgoyne dispatched Colonel Barry St. Leger with seven hundred regulars and loyalists, plus almost a thousand of the braves under the educated Mohawk, Joseph Brant, up the St. Lawrence to Lake Ontario. The general himself concentrated his main force at Fort St. John's on the Richelieu River (almost due east of Montreal) and embarked on June 15. Entering Lake Champlain, the army was rowed without resistance up the long lake in gunboats and Canadian boats called bateaux developed in the fur trade. They made a pretty picture on the water: dozens of large and small craft, colorful uniforms, sunlight flashing on musket barrels and wet paddles, bands playing. The flotilla approached Fort Ticonderoga on June 30. Burgoyne was fortunate to find the defending Americans crippled by quarreling commanders.

Schuyler, who had hardly distinguished himself in 1776, was, as might be expected of a second-rate, stubborn man, unwilling to resign his command of the Northern Department. New England militia especially objected to the wealthy landowner of New York. Congress ordered Gates back to lead the field army that was being raised, but he refused to serve under Schuyler. Major General Arthur St. Clair, a former British officer who had been with Washington at Trenton, was accordingly sent up and put in charge of Ticonderoga, now much strengthened by the young Polish engineer, Colonel Thaddeus Kosciuszko. This fort was expected to hold up the British by withstanding a siege for weeks. Yet St. Clair had only two thousand Continentals and three hundred artillerymen to man the stone fort, its outworks, and Mount Independence, across the narrows on the Vermont shore. Nine hundred militia were due daily. Behind Ticonderoga and to the southwest was a higher eminence, Mount Defiance, wild, heavily wooded, and unfortified.

Burgoyne split his advance forces, and Phillips, swinging west around Fort Ticonderoga, spotted Mount Defiance. "Where a goat can go, a man can go," he declared, "and where a man can go he can drag a gun." His engineers cut a path and hauled cannon up the slope on July 3 and 4, and Phillips pointed them down on Ticonderoga. St. Clair took the hint and evacuated the fort the next night, leaving immense stores and a hundred cannon. His troops crossed a bridge of boats to Mount Independence, picked up the troops there, and swung southward in a wide arc. Fraser and Riedesel gave chase, defeated a rear guard at Hubbardton (Vermont), and harried St. Clair all the way down to Fort Edward on the Hudson, a dilapidated old stockade halfway between Ticonderoga and Albany. Burgoyne overran Ticonderoga, established himself at Skenesborough, twenty-three miles above Fort Edward, and then took a rest for three weeks.

Washington was alarmed by this rapid advance and detached Major Generals Benedict Arnold and Benjamin Lincoln north with reinforcements. Lincoln was a Massachusetts farmer and politician of forty-four, heavily built, and a good steady soldier. Congress was disgusted with both St. Clair and Schuyler.

"A Thousand Untoward Circumstances"

It acted to remove the latter and ordered Gates up to assume full command. In the interim granted by Burgoyne, Schuyler moved up troops from Albany until he had forty-five hundred men. He set them to work felling trees in a tangled matting along the way that the British had to proceed. Great boulders were rolled down the hillsides into the creek crossings. New England militia began pouring in as word of Gates's coming spread; although he was from Virginia, they trusted him more than Schuyler.

The fatal delay of the British was owing to Burgoyne's insistence on advancing in force—infantry, forty-two cannon, wagons (including thirty carts with his own baggage and liquor), and women—all of which meant cutting a road through woods and over streams. He was oblivious to the need for haste. Besides, he was living in a loyalist's fine house and had found a pretty mistress in his entourage. Finally on July 24 he pushed forward fourteen miles to abandoned Fort Anne.

His Indians ranged out ahead on both sides. Near Fort Edward they came upon the cabin of a loyalist widow, Mrs. McNeil, a cousin of General Fraser. Visiting her was Jane McCrea, sister of a rebel but in love with a loyalist and former neighbor who was returning with Burgoyne's expedition. Reputedly beautiful, she at least was possessed of distinctively long hair, sometimes said to have been blonde. The Indians roughly seized both women and started in two parties back to the British camp. Mrs. McNeil arrived first and berated her cousin for this savage treatment. When the other party arrived, it escorted only Jane's unmistakable scalp. On the way the Indians had quarreled over their prize and killed, stripped, and mutilated her. Burgoyne demanded that her murderer be delivered up and sentenced him to death. A Canadian officer interceded and warned that the Indians would desert if the sentence was carried out. Burgoyne faltered and released the warrior, thereby incurring the sharp edge of this propaganda weapon. The story of the massacre and Burgoyne's condoning it spread rapidly through New York and New England. More and more militiamen turned their feet toward Albany. Even the New York loyalists wondered how safe they were from Burgoyne's undiscriminating savages. The killing of Jane McCrea, one of those vivid and magnified incidents of a campaign, passed into folklore and folk song, and the incrimination has blackened Burgoyne's name to this day.

The British finally reached Fort Edward on July 29. Schuyler had withdrawn down the Hudson twenty-five miles to Stillwater, where Kosciuszko laid out a defensive position to intrench. Burgoyne paused again, and here early in August he heard news both reassuring and ominous: St. Leger was approaching Fort Stanwix, one hundred miles west, but Howe was belatedly leaving New York headed south, blithely ignorant of any obligation to move up the Hudson unless Washington did. However, Burgoyne was not worried about himself.

Hearing of rebel supplies and horses gathered at Bennington, forty miles to the southeast, he dispatched Colonel Friedrich Baum on August 11 with 550 men to seize them. The German marched straight to his doom, for in the town there happened to be gathered 1,500 New Hampshire militia under Brigadier General John Stark, who had held the rail fence at Breed's Hill. Three days out Baum sighted militia in front of him and sent back for reinforcements. On August 16 Stark spread out his men to surround Baum. The latter saw these shirt-sleeved men on his flanks and assumed they must be loyalists coming to join him. He soon learned otherwise when Stark began his frontal attack.

"There they are!" he cried. "We'll beat them before night, or Molly Stark will be a widow."

Surrounded, Baum's men fought stubbornly but hopelessly; only nine of them escaped. In the afternoon 640 reinforcements under Colonel Heinrich von Breymann came near. Stark rounded up his men and moved forward to pitch into a second battle that soon saw Breymann fleeing west again. The battle of Bennington cost Burgoyne over two hundred killed and seven hundred prisoners, and staggered him. Stark lost thirty killed and forty wounded.

While Burgoyne rested at Fort Edward, Colonel St. Leger was in trouble. At Fort Oswego, New York, which he reached in mid-July, he was joined by over a hundred New York loyalists under Sir John Johnson, son of the late Sir William Johnson, long-time Crown superintendent of Indian affairs. The enmity between loyalists and patriots in upper and western New York was especially bitter, because the loyalists included royal officials who were able to turn the Iroquois, whom they had long supervised, against the frontier rebels. Political disagreement had rapidly degenerated into civil warfare with its attendant burning, plundering, and murder of neighbor against neighbor.

St. Leger's enlarged task force struck out eastward to attack old Fort Stanwix, now renamed Fort Schuyler (Rome, N.Y.). The garrison there amounted to seven hundred and fifty, but the commandant, Colonel Peter Gansevoort, daily expected a reinforcement of eight hundred under General Nicholas Herkimer, local landholder and son of a German immigrant. Informed of this coming reinforcement, Joseph Brant laid an ambush for Herkimer in a ravine near Oriskany. The Americans marched blindly into the trap on August 6 and then proceeded with bloody stubbornness to fight their way out. Losing an appalling 50 per cent of their men, they finally routed the Indians but gave up trying to reach the fort.

St. Leger laid siege to Fort Schuyler. Gansevoort got two men out during a night storm to seek help. They sped all the way to General Schuyler's headquarters, where Benedict Arnold offered to lead a relief column. He picked up a thousand volunteers eager to fight under him and hurried westward through the woods. In an effort to scare off St. Leger's Indian allies, Arnold sent on ahead a subnormal Dutchman who was well known to many of the Iroquois and acknowledged by them to be "touched" only by the Great Spirit. They regarded him with awe because of his dimwittedness. The Dutchman was instructed to report that an American force as numerous as the leaves on the trees was marching on Fort Schuyler. His undoubted story cooled the war fever of the braves, especially after their taste of resistance at Oriskany. Helping themselves to British liquor and clothing, they melted away into the forest. The loyalists, of no mind on second thought to face their infuriated neighbors, followed them. St. Leger's expedition was suddenly skeletonized to a remnant of regulars. He had no choice but to give up the siege on August 22 and withdraw to Oswego. This channel of Burgoyne's surge was dammed.

Gates now arrived at Stillwater and took over command. The American position had much improved in the past few weeks. Washington sent him Colonel Daniel Morgan's new corps of riflemen, and militia continued to march in. As soon as Arnold returned from his western triumph, Gates moved him six miles north to some higher ground called Bemis Heights, which Kosciuszko fortified. They were in no hurry to have Burgoyne advance, and he gave them plenty of time. It was September 13 before he had collected supplies for thirty days and was ready to get his heavy caravan in motion again. It took him five days to come in sight of Bemis Heights and mount an attack. He ordered three columns out the next morning under Riedesel, Fraser, and himself. Riedesel was to keep close to the river while Fraser and Burgoyne came together on the American left on the farm of one Isaac Freeman.

Watching the approach, Gates was content to wait in the fortifications. Impatient Arnold wanted to go out and meet the enemy in the woods of Freeman's farm, abandoning the advantage of the protected position. At length Gates let Arnold take Morgan's riflemen and Dearborn's New Hampshire regiment (three veterans together of the march to Quebec) and burst out against Fraser.[1] Arnold got into some difficulty, sent back for more regiments, and then sliced between Fraser and Burgoyne. The latter stood firm, but Arnold thought he could roll over Fraser. Gates refused his second plea for reinforcements, and at nightfall Arnold withdrew, fuming. Although the British remained on the battleground, they had lost nearly 600 men. Arnold's action had cost 320 Americans, 65 of them killed. Gates had been saved from an attack he might not have

---

1 James Wilkinson, Gates's adjutant, declared in a letter of September 21 that Arnold never was out of camp, and historians Bancroft and Channing accept this statement. Colonel Richard Varick and Colonel Henry B. Livingston wrote on September 22 and 23, respectively, to General Schuyler, each commenting on Arnold's activity in leading the troops. Lossing, Fiske, Wilson, Fortescue, and others accept these statements as reliable. Certainly inactivity during a battle does not coincide with Arnold's character. The controversy is ably discussed in Appendix II of Hoffman Nickerson, *The Turning Point of the Revolution* (Boston, 1928).

withstood and afterward had missed an opportunity to achieve a decisive victory. He did not mention Arnold in reporting the engagement, and the latter resented it in hot words. He asked to leave the area and was deprived of his command for insubordination. Fellow officers persuaded him not to resign, and he hung around in a long sulk, drawing to him the friends of Schuyler who resented Gates's ascendancy.

Lincoln then organized a strike far behind Burgoyne at Ticonderoga itself. His columns occupied Skenesboro, carried Mount Defiance and Mount Independence, but could not take the stout old stone fort. They took three hundred prisoners, released one hundred captured Americans, and generally gave Burgoyne the jitters. After the battle of September 19, his advance stalled again for two weeks, time he could not afford to lose because of the limited rations he carried. Gambler that he was, he decided to wait on the next word from General Clinton, who had sent him a message that he was about to strike up the Hudson from New York City.

HOWE MOVES TO PENNSYLVANIA

Sir William Howe's seaborne invasion was way off schedule. He pulled his last troops out of New Jersey early in July and put them on board transports. He left a garrison of seventy-two hundred in New York under Clinton, newly returned from England with a knighthood to mollify his smoldering resentment over the published version of the naval attack on Charleston. Howe finally sailed down the coast on July 23.

Storms and calms made a short voyage disagreeably long, and he finally landed at the head of Chesapeake Bay, fifty miles southwest of Philadelphia, on August 25. At sea he had received a further letter from Germain expressing the foolish hope that Howe's campaign would be finished in time to co-operate with Burgoyne's army! His fourteen thousand weary troops marched north and east to Brandywine Creek. They hardly endeared themselves to the rich countryside. Two of his men were hanged and five whipped for plundering. Howe's secretary noted that the "Hessians are more infamous and cruel than any. It is a misfortune we ever had such a dirty, cowardly set of contemptible miscreants."

Washington had marched his eleven thousand men from Morristown down to Philadelphia as soon as he could determine where Howe's transports were headed. He came up to the British in Delaware not far from their debarkation point and moved north in a parallel line with them to the Brandywine. Nathanael Greene wrote to his wife of this new theater of war:

Here are some of the most distressing scenes imaginable—the inhabitants generally desert their houses, furniture moving, cattle driving, and women and children travelling off on foot—the country all resounds with the cries of the people—the enemy plunders most amazingly.

The likeliest place for crossing the Brandywine was Chad's Ford, and here Washington put several brigades under Greene behind earthworks. Pennsylvania militia guarded his left, and Sullivan and Stirling commanded the right. The line was not unlike that on Long Island, outside Brooklyn, and Washington did not intend to let the enemy march around his flank as it had a year ago. This was the second pitched battle for him.

On September 11 Howe moved to cross the creek. Lieutenant General Baron Wilhelm von Knyphausen, the sixty-one-year-old commander of the Hessians, appeared at the ford late in the morning as if to engage Greene. Washington was sure this was not the main attack and soon heard that another body of the enemy had moved north. He sent a warning to Sullivan, but, seeing no one, that general concluded the information must be wrong. Howe was repeating his Long Island tactic, however, and he had started Cornwallis north at daybreak. His lordship marched so far that he crossed the Brandywine far beyond the American right. In fact when he turned back it took him until four o'clock in the the afternoon to make contact. Then with five thousand troops, Cornwallis overwhelmed the deceived Sullivan. Greene staved off defeat only by an extraordinary reversal of the Virginia Continentals. He pulled them out of line, marched four miles through broken country in fifty minutes, and held Cornwallis at bay while the whole American army pulled back under cover of darkness to Chester. Howe suffered ninety killed and almost five hundred wounded, but Washington is believed to have lost three hundred killed, probably six hundred wounded, and four hundred prisoners. The Americans had been outgeneraled, but Washington defended Sullivan when Congress tried to break him.

All organization shattered, the men flowed in the direction of Chester, companies, regiments, and brigades fragmented and intermingled. How far they might have marched is uncertain. But on the east side of Chester Creek stood a French youth of nineteen who, with a small guard, brought the retreat to a halt. He was a volunteer without rank and wore a hasty bandage around one leg. His name was long and noble, but the men knew him simply as "Lafayette."

Only Greene's division came up unbroken, and Washington with it. Then began the sorting out of the men and the restoring of units. It was a curious sort of withdrawal, without

panic. Captain Enoch Anderson wrote that he heard no de-
spairing remarks. "We had our solacing words already for
each other—'Come, boys, we shall do better another time.'"

In the next week the American army retreated to the Schuylkill River on the edge of Philadelphia, swung north, and darted
west to make an attack that was drowned out in torrential
rains that soaked their powder. Brigadier General Anthony
Wayne was left near Paoli, where he had lived as a boy, with
fifteen hundred men to threaten Howe's left. He lay hidden
in a wood and thought his presence was unknown, but loyalists
carried the news to the British. On the night of September 20
one of Howe's subordinates, Lord Grey, led a bayonet attack
on Wayne, inflicting two hundred to three hundred casualities
and taking seventy-one prisoners. Howe then advanced to a
position between Washington and the Quaker city, and Congress was warned to flee. It adjourned to York, and Howe
entered the capital on September 26.

Washington was not through yet. Reinforcements came to
him that restored his army to more than eleven thousand. He
returned toward Germantown, north of Philadelphia, where
Howe had stationed without intrenchments his main force of
less than nine thousand. Their line extended about three miles
east from the Schuylkill. Washington's troops were stretched
out for seven miles west to east. But there were four roads
running southward, converging gradually as they entered or
passed Germantown. Washington planned to march his men
down those four roads on the night of October 3 so that they
would hit the British at dawn simultaneously on both flanks
and at two places frontally. The four columns were to be led
by Sullivan, Greene, John Armstrong, and William Smallwood.
The directions on how to keep to the main roads were sketchy

at best. Co-ordination is difficult to achieve at night and no maneuver for half-trained troops. This kind of wide-jawed pincer movement had ancient precedents, but in those maneuvers the outside lines were made up of the strongest forces. Washington put his heaviest strength in the two center columns.

A drop in temperature raised a heavy fog late at night. Nevertheless, the attack began well with surprise. Sullivan hit first and rolled the enemy back. Some delay occurred when the British held a stone house like a fortress, and Washington finally left a detachment to contain the place while the column pressed on. Meanwhile, Greene was delayed half an hour by a bewildered guide. While he was hurrying into action, his right wing under Adam Stephen, who had been drinking, mistook Sullivan's left in the fog for the enemy and opened fire on Wayne's men. Discovery of this bloody error broke up both divisions. Yet when Greene's main ramming force struck, he broke the British line, smashed into town, and engaged in bloody house-to-house fighting. Victory was in sight, but there was no pressure on the British flanks. Armstrong had been too easily turned back, and Smallwood had not arrived.

Cornwallis came running out of Philadelphia with reinforcements; Grant drove some troops between Sullivan and Greene. The sound of firing on all sides, plus the fog, seems to have confused the Americans and, as Washington reported, "when every thing gave the most flattering hopes of victory, the troops began suddenly to retreat." It was a heartbreaking outcome. Even Howe's dog got confused in the mist and followed the retreating Americans. Washington returned him under a flag of truce.

All the American generals were disappointed and angered

by the turn of events at Germantown, principally because they were puzzled by it. Wayne was caustic: "We ran from Victory." While Howe suffered 100 killed and 420 wounded, Washington counted 152 killed, 521 wounded, and 400 captured. Stephen was court-martialed for his blunder and dismissed from the service. Washington was criticized in Congress, his performance soon contrasted with Gates's at Saratoga.

SARATOGA

With the exciting prospect of Clinton stabbing the Americans in the back, Burgoyne deluded himself and gambled away sixteen precious days in idleness against his dwindling provisions. Clinton did make a thrust up the river (Howe's parting suggestion), but he was as cautious as Burgoyne was reckless. Delaying until he received reinforcements from England, he seized Forts Montgomery and Clinton from Putnam's command and reached West Point on October 8. The messengers between Clinton and Burgoyne were frequently captured. Burgoyne could not learn exactly where Clinton was or how fast he was moving. On his part, Clinton was disconcerted to hear from Burgoyne's last messenger, October 5, that the distressed commander was soliciting *orders* from Clinton, a deft shifting of responsibility for the outcome of a dubious operation. Clinton quickly eluded this yoke and returned to New York City. His subordinate, Major General John Vaughan, pushed northward and burned Kingston on October 15. He was only forty-five miles below Albany, but time had run out.

Gradually Burgoyne realized that time was all in Gates's favor. Besides his casualties, he had lost other soldiers by desertion and almost all his Indians. Already he was outnumbered: fifty-two hundred to the Americans' seven thousand, plus twenty-five hundred militia that had recently moved up behind him. The strain from nightly harassment and from summer clothing in the cold fall was telling on his men; yet he had to put them on half-rations on October 3. He called a council of war to which he proposed an all-out attack on Gates's left by a wide sweep through the woods. The realistic Riedesel recommended retreat until the army was within reach of Lake Champlain, where it could embark if necessary or advance again when Clinton reached Albany. Fraser agreed with him; Phillips said nothing. Burgoyne declared that retreat was disgraceful but finally consented to modify his offensive move. On October 7 he put sixteen hundred and fifty of his troops in motion with ten cannon to strike at the American left. It was an uncertain, even pointless reconnaissance in force. At least there was no lack of command, for the four generals accompanied this detachment. The column proceeded slowly less than a mile beyond their intrenchments and then drew up in a long line on open ground.

As soon as Gates learned of the approach he accepted the enticing invitation to attack, for a woods at either end of Burgoyne's line provided cover for flank advances safe from cannon. "Order on Morgan to begin the game," he said. Hardbitten, easy moving Dan Morgan led his rifle corps around through the woods to fire on Burgoyne's right. Enoch Poor's brigade was to strike his left. When these two were in position, Ebenezer Learned's brigade would take on the center. Gates stayed at his headquarters throughout the battle, which was proper if not inspiring. Hearing the musket fire, Arnold could not stand inaction. He forgot his pique, leaped on his horse, and galloped out of camp. Gates sent an aide in pursuit to order him back.

Suddenly Arnold appeared at the head of Learned's Connecticut troops waving his sword and shouting, a dynamic personality of tremendous military reputation and popularity. He was the spark that ignited the American attack. The men cheered and surged against Burgoyne's Germans. Poor had already chewed up the grenadiers on the British left, and Morgan's riflemen were knocking over the light infantry on the right. Fraser was mortally wounded. Burgoyne ordered a retreat to the fortified lines. This withdrawal, however, did not break off the battle. Arnold scooped up all the loose troops he could find and pressed a further attack. The Americans were also immensely heartened by the arrival of three thousand Albany militia.

Burgoyne's foolishness had released a swarm of hornets. He needed luck now to save his army. His disorganized detachment did not get back into the redoubts they normally held. Arnold was on their heels, a fighting fool leading a charmed life, once galloping down between the two lines of fire to reach a party of Morgan's riflemen. These he led boldly against the first redoubt, held by Colonel von Breymann and his surviving Germans. Frantic and tyrannical, the Brunswicker beat his men to make them hold on, until one of them turned and shot him dead. Then they gave up the redoubt, but their last volley killed Arnold's horse and broke the general's leg, the same one wounded at Quebec. The way was open, however, to carry Burgoyne's whole position. Gates committed no more men to the attack and was not in a position to see the advantage given him. When Arnold lay on the ground, immobile at last, Gates's aide reached him with orders to return to camp. The fire went out of the American attack and night descended. Thus ended the second battle of Freeman's Farm, or of Bemis Heights as it is also known. Gates suffered only 150 casualties in the late afternoon drubbing given the enemy. He did give Arnold much credit in his report, and Burgoyne gave him all.

The captured redoubt was held, and next day Burgoyne knew he must move. In the harvests of Freeman's Farm he had lost not only two good officers but nearly one thousand men. He ordered a retreat, leaving five hundred sick and wounded behind. Heavy clouds opened and rain poured down. After three days of intermittent slogging through mud, the weary troops reached Saratoga (Schuylerville, N.Y.), only seven miles to the north. Attracted by the comforts of the Schuyler mansion, Burgoyne ordered a halt. American militia lay ahead of him and across the river, too. With the British lion wounded and at bay, Gates's army swelled in the next ten days to seventeen thousand hunters ready for the kill.

Completely surrounded and dispirited, Burgoyne asked Gates for terms on October 13. The latter required unconditional surrender, when he should have demanded that Burgoyne propose terms which he would modify or accept. As a result, haggling went on for four days, and when Burgoyne boasted that he had "succeeded to dictate every term" he was correct. He did not so much capitulate as reach an agreement, or convention, by which he gave up not his men but their arms; the men were to march to a port, embark for England, and not serve again in North America. The terms were generous to a fault, for Burgoyne's men would simply release other British troops for service in America, as Washington pointed out to

Congress. So the "convention army" was kept near Boston throughout the winter, then marched to Virginia for safer keeping, and never sent home. One result was that hundreds deserted to begin a new and better life on the frontier.

Before Congress is condemned for breaching an agreement that ought not to have been made, the reader should know that Howe promptly sent secret word to Burgoyne that once he got his men on transports the Germans might return to England, but the three thousand British troops should be brought around to New York for reassignment! In consequence of this order, Burgoyne and his men sought every opportunity to provoke their American guards into some illegal act that he could use later to justify his planned violation of the convention.

An actor to the last, Burgoyne seemed to enjoy playing his role of defeated general and "guest" of Gates. "The fortune of war has made me your prisoner," he announced when he met Gates. Schuyler came up for the ceremony and Burgoyne was embarrasssed to confess he had burned the former's house. He got off a letter to Clinton that began with a dramatic flourish:

After two very sharp actions, infinite fatigue, disappointment of intelligence from you, & a thousand other untoward circumstances, I was compelled to fall back to Saratoga.

And for three pages a play-by-play account of the proceedings was narrated. At length he admitted surrender and then struck a pose of martyred valor:

I have had some narrow personal escapes, having been shot through my hat & waistcoat, & my horse hit, in the last action. If my reputation suffers among the respectable part of my profession, I shall think those escapes unfortunate.

It did and they were. He made his exit from the military stage unmourned, unhonored, and unsung. His very own blunders and ill-judgments had rung down the curtain.

PHILADELPHIA

Howe was not safely ensconced in Philadelphia yet. He had to rely on ships for supplies, and the Americans still held the lower Delaware—held it with two forts, floating batteries, and *chevaux-de-frise* (sharpened stakes held on the bottom in iron sockets and pointed upward at an angle so as to puncture ship hulls). Howe pulled his men out of Germantown and called for help from his brother, the admiral. A joint attack on Fort Mercer, at Red Bank, New Jersey, cost Colonel von Donop his life along with more than three hundred casualties and two ships, without success. Colonel Christopher Greene, who had marched with Arnold to Quebec, was the stubborn defender, commanding only four hundred men.

That same day, October 22, Howe was writing a long letter to Lord Germain. He had heard of Burgoyne's retreat, but he discounted rebel rumors of his surrender. Anticipating criticism, he expressed surprise to hear that Burgoyne had "expected a co-operating army at Albany." Bluntly confessing that there was "no prospect of terminating the war to the advantage of Great Britain" in the present campaign, Howe expatiated on plans for the next, making impossible demands: ten thousand men for New England, fifteen thousand for the South, garrisons to hold New York and Philadelphia, etc. Then he abruptly changed his tone.

From the little attention, my Lord, given to my Recommendations since the commencement of my command, I am led to hope I may be relieved from this very painful Service, wherein I have not the good fortune to enjoy the necessary confidence and Support of my Superiors.

Howe knew he had failed, both as a peacemaker and as a conqueror, and he was going to get his resignation in before news of Burgoyne's surrender should reach London.

Next the British turned their attention to Fort Mifflin on Mud Island, Pennsylvania, and, with naval guns mounted on shore, shelled it for five days. The surviving half of the small garrison escaped to Colonel Greene in Fort Mercer. So Cornwallis led two thousand troops against the stronghold in a second assault on November 10. Greene at last abandoned the fort and got away safely, having "sold" his position at an exorbitant price.

Howe was now secure in the rebel capital. With its forty thousand population, Philadelphia was also the largest city in America—indeed, it was larger than any city in England except London. Therefore its capture seemed like an important victory. But what had Howe won? Washington's army stood intact at the north portal when it should have been destroyed. Indeed, the benefit of his holding Washington away from Burgoyne had been negated by the rise of a second army at Stillwater. The total number of Americans under arms was temporarily larger than it ever had been, and units from Gates's command were now joining Washington.

The loyalists alleged to populate southeastern Pennsylvania failed to appear after the plundering marches of the British and Germans. Some of the people tried to be neutral, but many of them were pacifistic Quakers, of no use to the invader beyond serving as suppliers. And all of this year's effort had wound up by costing a British army at Saratoga. Any hope once held of cutting off supplies to Washington's army disappeared. Small wonder that Howe settled down in the city with his mistress and his gambling cronies for an agreeable winter until his resignation should be accepted.

Neither Howe nor Washington was aware that the character of the war was changing that winter. The miscarriage of British plans for the campaign of 1777 meant far more than the failure of the biggest offensive the colonial office had put together; it signaled the impossibility of ever trying it again under circumstances so favorable, because the first failure encouraged France and her friends to intervene openly on the side of the Americans. A colonial rebellion was merging into a world war.

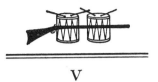

V

Disappointments in Battle and Alliance

If Washington reviewed his situation in the Valley Forge winter of 1777–78—and surely he did—he must have realized that his Fabian tactics were not winning the war. That is not to say that they were fruitless—or that he had a choice. They had staved off defeat, and this was a major achievement. Three British generals had gone down in failure: one recalled, one captured, one resigned. Yet for Washington almost three years of conflict had passed in a seesawing motion—a victory here, a defeat there, up and down. The end was not in sight.

This pattern was duplicated in his army, which fluctuated from small to large and small again. Only in part had he been able to lick the problem of short enlistments. Not until the latter part of 1776 had Congress authorized enlistments for three years or the duration of the war, accompanying this contract with a twenty-dollar bounty, a new suit of clothes each year, and a land grant of one hundred acres to the ranks. In reality the clothes seldom were issued and the pay fell months behind. Since state militias offered twenty to thirty dollars for short enlistments, many men preferred to stay out of the Continental army and rally to the colors only when the fighting rolled into their own state. Consequently, Washington seldom could get numerical superiority to or even equality with the enemy, except under the most threatening crisis when he could no longer mount an offensive. Among Americans consuming fear of a large professional army doomed him to reliance on state militia for adequate numbers.

Washington's immediate problem was to supply the army he did have. Beyond that, to drive out the invaders he needed two kinds of aid: sea power and expert technical advice in military engineering, training, and ordnance production. For these he had to look for foreign help.

When the American army determined on winter quarters at Valley Forge, twenty-two miles northwest of Philadelphia, it was compromising between a winter campaign (which Pennsylvania wanted) and camping in Delaware (which Pennsylvania resisted). Campaigning was impossible because the troops were virtually immobilized by insufficient clothing. Washington reported to Congress on December 23, 1777, that there were twenty-nine hundred men "unfit for duty because they were bare foot and otherwise naked." By February 5 the number in such condition had increased to four thousand. For those lucky enough to have any, blankets served as coats. The able-bodied who had clothes raced to build huts to save the naked and the ill. Meanwhile they all fought the cold and vermin. Soap was almost unobtainable. At one time no meat was available for issue for six days; on three occasions the camp ran out of provisions. Five hundred horses starved to death. Small-pox and typhus kept the hospitals in neighboring communities full. Men died at the rate of four hundred a month. Nor were all the troops steadfast: hundreds deserted either to go home or to join the British.

The causes of this acute distress were primarily mismanagement, graft, speculation, and selfishness. The weather could not have been helped; the lack of supplies could have been. Congress had created a commissary department and a quartermaster department and set forth regulations. The former was to procure food, and it functioned fairly well until the appointment of a new commissary general in the spring of 1777; William Buchanan was simply unequal to his duties, and procurement fell off all summer and fall. Congress authorized Washington to commandeer harvests, but he disliked using such power. Finally in December Congress ordered him to seize foodstuffs in the area. After Jeremiah Wadsworth was appointed commissary general, he got food and brought it into Valley Forge, but by then a winter of near starvation had passed.

Clothing and forage were the principal concern of the quartermaster department. Quartermaster General Thomas Mifflin had resigned in November, 1777, after several months away from the army. The trickle of supplies came to a standstill, and Congress unbelievably left the post vacant for three months! After a committee visited Valley Forge, it recommended the obvious: appointment of a capable new quartermaster general and adoption of new regulations. Nathanael Greene was persuaded to take the hopeless job. He and his two assistants were allowed, according to the military custom, to divide 1 per cent of all funds issued by their department for their pay. By vigorous attention to duty Greene found clothing and other supplies. He was discouraged at times by scandalous quality in fabric and leather, and he had to range far for forage. Uniforms Congress had ordered from France finally arrived in June, 1778, but the army was not well clothed until the following November.

The Valley Forge winter was not the coldest of the war; the next season of 1779–80 was to be more biting and to see much more snow. It was not the most discouraging winter; morale had sunk lower in December, 1776, when it seemed that the Revolution might collapse. The troops at Valley Forge were not so much despondent about their fighting qualities as they were sick, and they were wrathful at Congress for failing to satisfy their physical wants. Possibly twenty-five hundred perished during the six months in camp. No other winter exacted such a toll. As a century passed, their suffering took on a virtuous hue and was made responsible for the forging of a stronger army. The analogy of applying heat to metal to harden it is not a suitable one. The army was stronger in the spring simply because it received some sensible training, recruiting continued, the fainthearted had deserted, and the sick had either died or recovered. It would have been still stronger if it could have received the food and clothing that Congress bungled in providing and civilians selfishly withheld.

Congress, indeed, had been busy strengthening the political unity of the colonies, already functioning under new state constitutions. After sixteen months of debate the delegates in November, 1777, had hammered out the Articles of Confederation describing a union of states. Calculated to preserve the liberties which were, according to the Declaration of Independence, transgressed, these Articles were a written constitution that created a "perpetual union." Congress was to remain the single agency of government; each state was to have one vote, although the number of delegates varied; and revenue was to be contributed by the states in proportion to their land values. The document had now gone to the states for ratification, and by the summer of 1778 nine would have adopted it. Independence was solidifying, although Maryland's objection to the omission of western boundaries for the states that extended vaguely westward prevented the Articles from going into effect until 1781.

JEALOUS GENERALS

As if Washington did not have pressing enough problems that winter, the forced assimiliation of foreign volunteers finally brough on military indigestion. Soldiers of fortune were not uncommon in Europe, and the war in America brought numerous applicants to our commissioners in France. They began arriving in America in 1776. With European disdain for colonial troops, they wanted and expected to be generals. A few condescended to take rank as lieutenant colonels or captains. Some were opportunists seeking glory abroad for promotion at home, without concern for the issues of the war. Others were hardheaded, competent professionals who lacked a war in Europe in which to practice their special knowledge. Only a few became interested in this burgeoning republic with its advanced ideas about human freedom.

Among them were overrated officers like Roche de Fermoy, who simply lacked capacity and resigned. There were arrogant trouble-makers like Philippe du Coudray (who, before he could antagonize many, foolishly rode his horse onto a ferry, across the deck, into the river, and drowned) and like Thomas Conway (who did not). Then there were stalwarts, the talented men who gave the American army a tremendous lift by their expert knowledge: the group of French engineers headed by Louis Duportail, a colonel who rose by Washington's recommendations to major general; Johann Kalb, self-styled baron, a perceptive Bavarian in the French service who lost his life in action here; and the Marquis de Fleury, Mauduit du Plessis, Charles Armand-Tufin, and Anne Louis de Tousard, men who could and would fight. Others were yet to come. Surpassing them all was the incredible Marquis de Lafayette, wealthy idealist, who worshipped Washington and captivated everyone by his wide-eyed charm, including the men he led as a youthful major general. He was wounded at Germantown and endured the winter at Valley Forge. Sticking it out to the end, he twice revisited this country and received the homage of a grateful nation.

Two Poles came—Thaddeus Kosciuszko and Count Casimir Pulaski—from a land just overrun by Prussia, Russia, and Austria and divided among them. Kosciuszko was an able engineer who arrived in 1776, fought in the Saratoga campaign, and served to the close of the war. Pulaski, twenty-nine in 1777, was made a cavalry commander and died of wounds at Savannah in 1779. Both men have left their names on towns and counties across the country.

Finally, there appeared early in 1778 the ambitious and unemployed Prussian, Baron Friedrich von Steuben, two years older than Washington and a former staff captain under Frederick the Great. Franklin elevated him to the rank of Frederick's "lieutenant general" so that Steuben would get the respect his considerable knowledge and talents deserved. Amazingly adaptable, he modified the Prussian training methods that were the envy of Europe and devised a drill system for America that remained standard for years. Handicapped only by a profound shortage of English, Steuben began formal military training of the troops late in February, 1778, by speaking French to interpreters who translated his shouts for him. At night he composed a manual which was translated and copied for the benefit of the officers. For the first time the army was getting uniform and effective training in arms, and getting it from officers rather than sergeants. Steuben had a happy faculty for making the men like him even when he berated them for their stupidity and indifference. One of his outbursts to an interpreter, sounding like that of a dialect comedian, is still recalled:

"Viens, Walker, mon ami, mon bon ami! Sacré! Goddam de gaucheries of dese badauts! Je ne puis plus. I can curse dem no more!"

Thomas Conway, already mentioned, was an Irish Catholic reared in France. To advance himself from major in the French army he came over in 1776 at the age of forty-three and was appointed a brigadier general in May, 1777. He was a good officer, but he was also a sensitive faultfinder and talked too freely. He pestered Congress to promote him to the rank of major general, because Kalb had been, and was almost successful until Washington remonstrated. All the foreign officers created problems of rank and disappointment for Americans who might be equally deserving. After Gates's victory, Conway wrote the general a laudatory letter, asked to serve under him, and added, "Heaven has been determined to save your country, or a weak General and bad counsellors would have ruined it."

Gates's aide saw the letter and quoted the passage to a fellow officer; it was repeated to General Stirling, who forwarded the quotation to Washington. The latter sent off a curt note to Conway, November 9, 1777, repeating the quotation, and the fat was in the fire. Since he could not deny it, Conway tried to explain it away with insincere persiflage. When Gates heard of the exchange, he wrote to Washington demanding to know who had been spying on his correspondence. Learning ultimately that it was his own aide, he almost fought a duel with him.

Coincident with this personal controversy, Congress reconstituted the Board of War and named the victorious Gates president. In a technical sense this appointment elevated him above Washington. Then the board recommended Conway to the new office of inspector general. He showed up at Valley Forge, where he got a chilly reception, and returned to Congress. Sent off to the Hudson, he fulminated and threatened to resign, a gesture Congress promptly accepted. Steuben was made inspector general, a much more sensible choice.

The whole episode, sometimes called the Conway Cabal, was not a conspiracy by which Gates sought to replace Washington as commander-in-chief. There may have been Congressmen who considered that possibility, but Gates was innocent of collusion, although he handled himself poorly in explaining Conway's letter to Washington, just as he had snubbed him earlier by reporting Burgoyne's surrender directly to Congress. The incident did snap Washington's enormous patience, for the insult came at a time when he had been rubbed by congressional criticism, disappointment in two battles, the culmination of foreign self-seeking, and the breakdown in supplies for his army. He was soon working smoothly with Gates again, although they never became warm friends.

Disappointments in Battle and Alliance

The winter of Valley Forge brought to a climax the French policy of unofficial aid to America. Ever since 1763 France had smarted over England's superiority. The expense of her colonies in the West Indies had rather dampened her desire to recover Canada, but she was hurt by her loss of prestige and influence in European affairs. She wanted to humiliate England and see her empire reduced. Believing that her old enemy's position was founded on her commerce, France considered that the loss of the American colonies would ruin England's trade and reduce her prestige. In devotion to revenge, the Comte de Vergennes, foreign minister, blinded himself to the perception that the revolution he wanted to support was a contagious flame that might consume his master, Louis XVI. Both should have had warning from the popularity of the American cause with the French people.

The French government secretly supplied the capital by which Caron de Beaumarchais, playwright and enthusiastic friend of America, established a trading company that shipped clothing, arms, powder, and medicines to the colonies. Vergennes opened French ports to American privateers, allowing those vessels to make repairs, take on supplies, and dispose of prize ships. Ports in the French West Indies were used as points for transshipping goods brought safely that far across the Atlantic. And, of course, French officers were allowed to serve in the American army. Meanwhile, France was building up its navy, keeping a large British fleet in home waters.

The astute Vergennes, carefully playing his game of international poker, feared only two eventualities: either that the United States and England would reconcile by agreement or by defeat of the former, or that England might strike at France without warning, as she had in 1756, to stop the naval rivalry. Therefore, Vergennes intended to supply enough aid to insure that the United States would not give up the revolution and yet not enough to antagonize England into military reprisal. His hand of cards was not easily vulnerable. He recognized that Britain would have to endure France's evasion of her obligations as a neutral because she did not want a second war on her hands right away. Both nations could pretend ignorance of the secret aid, but by 1777 the "business" carried on by American privateers in French ports advertised England's impotence to the world. With news of Burgoyne's steady advance and Howe's victories, the English ambassador lodged a veiled threat with Vergennes. The foreign minister grew uneasy as the summer of 1777 ended. He ordered privateers out of French ports, stopped the loading of ships bound for America, and announced that captured British ships brought into French harbors would be restored to their owners. His move to appease England reckoned not with the resources of the American commissioner to France—Benjamin Frankin.

Franklin had been sent to the court of France late in 1776 to secure French aid in the form of gifts, loans, and purchases. Congress had been reluctant heretofore to seek a political alliance with the colonies' traditional enemy. Now Franklin bent his efforts to pulling France into the war as an active partner with its navy and army. Although handicapped by his fellow commissioners, Arthur Lee and Silas Deane, the very souls of badgering tactlessness, Franklin charmed everyone as the brilliant scientist and genial philosopher. He also knew how to play a game of bluff. If Vergennes was now anxious about England, he should be made anxious about America as well. Franklin started a rumor that he was leaving Paris—since there was nothing more to be done diplomatically—and would go to London. He let himself be seen talking to Englishmen. He spoke of the virtues of self-reliance: would it not be better for the United States to avoid any alliance and the consequent obligations to another nation? After all, could a monarchy be expected to encourage a republic?

Vergennes began to sweat. He let Franklin know that the restrictions he had imposed were temporary—as indeed they were. When news came of Burgoyne's surrender, he opened the French ports again in defiance of humbled England. But the American victory also suggested to Vergennes that Britain might well propose attractive terms of reconciliation to bring the war to an end. He therefore urged his king to offer an alliance to the Americans so as to keep them fighting. Louis XVI, who preferred repairing clocks to state affairs, had grown less interested in humiliating England than he was in avoiding the cost of warfare. Besides, he had faith in his uncle, Charles III of Spain, and would be guided by his position.

So Vergennes sought to embroil Spain, too. She had already contributed to Beaumarchais's company so that it could buy supplies for America and then set up a trading company at home. But a new Spanish foreign minister, the Conde de Floridablanca, was not going to be led into war by France. He wanted England and the United States to exhaust each other; therefore he was willing to give secret aid. He was upset by Burgoyne's defeat, always fearful that Spain's restive colonies might be encouraged to revolt. It was true that Spain wanted to win back Gibraltar and Minorca from the English, but not at the expense and risk of war just now.

Vergennes's assessment of England's position was correct.

The War for Independence

Burgoyne's defeat was a staggering blow, after the immoderate rejoicing over his easy capture of Fort Ticonderoga. Howe's request to resign signified not only that he considered the year's campaign a waste but that he saw no victory he could gain in the future. Since the strategy had been planned in London and failure was largely owing to Germain's not clarifying the plans and co-ordinating the armies, the responsibility sat ghoulishly in the ministry's lap. Lord North, who led the King's administration as prime minister, begged to resign. The King refused him, just as he refused to accept Howe's resignation immediately. He wanted time to find reasonable hope for his stubbornness. The Whig opposition rejoiced at the embarrassment of the King's friends. Chatham, Fox, Shelburne, Rockingham, and Burke were jubilant, sarcastic, and accusatory. They called again for making peace.

In the face of such strengthened opposition, George III encouraged Lord North to reverse himself. Thus he stood up in Parliament in December, 1777, and announced that after the Christmas recess he would offer a plan for peace. If this switch exasperated the Whigs by stealing their platform, it confirmed Vergennes's worst fear. While the British Parliament took its usual recess from December 11 to January 20, 1778, in spite of such a crisis, Vergennes "persuaded" Franklin to enter into an alliance.

The formal documents (commercial and military) were not ready for signing until February 6. Not only did France become the first to recognize the infant country, but she renounced all claims to North America east of the Mississippi. She might, however, enlarge her holdings in the West Indies at Britain's expense. Neither country was to lay down its arms until the independence of the United States was assured (this to prevent reconciliation with England). The alliance was still secret, not to go into effect until England should declare war on France. Vergennes announced to the British government on March 12 only the treaty of commerce, and a week later Franklin and his colleagues were formally received at Versailles by Louis XVI as representatives of a sovereign power. Congress ratified the treaties on May 4, and the news was celebrated at Valley Forge next day.

Even though spies brought reliable rumors of the military alliance to London, Lord North proceeded in a leisurely manner in February, 1778, to implement his announced policy. He offered too little much too late. The ministry called for repeal of the old tea tax and the other "intolerable" acts, authorized a commission of negotiators to go to America, and yet strengthened its military position. The commission was headed by the young and earnest Frederick Howard, Earl of Carlisle, and included William Eden, a diplomat of some experience, and George Johnstone, an empty-minded, litigious ex-governor of West Florida. The commission could treat with anyone and offer virtual home rule, but it could not recognize independence or agree to withdraw the military forces. It was doomed, of course, before it started, and it did not set out until the middle of April. It is to be wondered what North or the King expected from the commission, beyond stilling momentarily the clamor of the Whig opposition.

Meanwhile, the bewildered Germain had tried to think up some instructions for the inactive army. Howe had made no attempt, which might easily have been successful, to gather in Washington's hungry, paralyzed scarecrows at nearby Valley Forge. As spring came on he was needled by a loyalist versifier:

The War for Independence

Awake, arouse, Sir Billy,
There's forage in the plain,
Ah, leave your little Filly,
And open the campaign.

But Sir William had virtually seceded from the war until he could go home. The King finally accepted his resignation and appointed Sir Henry Clinton to the command. Clinton suggested raiding the New England coast to reduce shipbuilding and privateering. But when the French alliance became public news, George III wrote personally and ordered Clinton to evacuate Philadelphia, possibly New York, but to hold Newport; he was to send five thousand of his troops to attack the French West India island of St. Lucia, and three thousand to Florida for another expedition. Strategy was taking a sharp turn southward, and the army was to be subordinated to the navy.

These orders were more than enough to traumatize the overly cautious Clinton, but the irony of the situation was that the Carlisle commission was kept ignorant of them because the retreat from Philadelphia would leave the commission no point of strength from which to negotiate! Here was the kind of muddle that George III excelled at compounding. North asked again and again to resign, but the King had tied him with bribes and could not stand the sight of any of the Whig leaders, even after Chatham died.

News of what the Carlisle commission would offer had preceded its arrival, and the terms were rejected. Bad as the war was, almost no American would settle now for less than independence. Moreover, the army, or most of it, had survived the Valley Forge winter, and now, with Steuben's training, the French alliance, and Howe's removal, the outlook was cheerful and exciting once more. When the Carlisle commission finally reached Philadelphia in June, it found Howe gone and Clinton on hand making plans to move the army back to New York. Carlisle and his colleagues were infuriated by this royal betrayal, but requested a hearing before Congress. The latter refused until either independence was recognized or the military forces withdrawn from the country. Since the commission had now exhausted its pathetic role, it retired to New York with the departing army. Subsequently it tried bribery and broadsides, only to be ridiculed for its puny efforts.

CLASH AT MONMOUTH

Clinton sent off three thousand loyalists and some unreliable Germans by water on Admiral Howe's transports. The rest of the army, about ten thousand, he marched across New Jersey, leaving Philadelphia on June 18. Washington detached a brigade under the convalescing Arnold to occupy the city and then took off in eager pursuit of Clinton.

The Americans sang "Yankee Doodle" and other airs as they marched. Since Clinton was moving northeast and they were going more directly east, it was certain that the armies would meet somewhere in northern New Jersey. With great confidence in his revitalized army, Washington was more ready than his officers for a showdown battle. Charles Lee, recently exchanged, led the advance at his own request. He had been reluctant to bring on a battle, so Washington gave him direct orders to attack. Early on June 28 Clinton was overtaken near Monmouth Court House, and he turned six thousand of his men, infantry and cavalry, to beat off Lee's approaching van of fifty-four hundred. The second division, under Washington, was several miles behind. The mercury was rising toward 100 degrees.

The War for Independence

In preparation the night before, Lee had issued no instructions to the brigadiers and ordered no reconnaissance. He said he had no plan and would rely on them to act as circumstances dictated. Consequently, the moves that developed were uncoordinated. The several brigades were not in any order or line of battle when the fighting began. The brigadiers (Lafayette, Wayne, William Maxwell, Charles Scott, and James M. Varnum) issued orders and so did Lee, with the result that there were irregular advances and withdrawals. Sharp fighting by detachments ended in retreat for lack of support. As the confused units fell back, Clinton exerted more pressure. The sweating Continentals in a swelling exodus tramped nearly three miles across two ravines toward Washington's support. Lee rode with them.

When Washington heard of the retreat he rode forward in disbelief. He questioned the first regiments he saw, but they could not explain their flight except that they had had orders—or no orders. Finally Washington came up to Lee.

"I desire to know, sir, what is the reason, whence arises all this confusion?"

More was said, but reports vary. If Washington did not swear at Lee, he certainly berated him for his poor performance and failure to press the attack. He stopped the retreat, reformed the units as they came up, added some reinforcements, and prepared a line of battle. The British were already attacking, but an American front was taking shape and holding. For a good hour cannon and muskets kept up an incessant fire. The spring's training showed in the steadiness of the men under coordinated direction. Clinton threw his best men at the left of the line and then at the right. When he found he was hammering against a stone wall, he broke off the action. It was late afternoon, and the thirst of the panting men on both sides was feathering their mouths. A lull of more than an hour ensued. Clinton launched another attack that was beaten off. Cannonading persisted for a while, and then about six o'clock the British pulled back a mile. Washington tried to organize an attack, but by the time he got fresh regiments forward it was too near dusk to risk an engagement.

The battle concluded indecisively, and before dawn the British moved on, leaving their wounded behind. Washington counted 69 Americans killed, 161 wounded, and 131 missing, of which at least 37 were later found dead of sunstroke. Even Washington's horse dropped dead. Clinton reported 147 dead, 170 wounded, and 64 missing, but American burial parties buried 251 British and Germans! In addition, Clinton also lost 600 deserters, mostly Germans, during his long march.

On balance Clinton could say he had fended off an attack and carried his army safely to New York, as ordered. Washington, deprived of a victory he should have enjoyed, could argue that he held the battleground and had inflicted more casualties than he had suffered. Lee wanted a court-martial for what he considered unmerited rebuke, and he got it. He was found guilty of disobeying orders and of making an unnecessary retreat and was removed from command for one year. Afterward, being unwilling to serve, this vastly overrated problem child was dismissed from the service.

Washington rested his army, then marched up to the Hudson and encamped at White Plains. "It is not a little pleasing," he wrote, "nor less wonderful to contemplate, that after two years Manoeuvring . . . both Armies are brought back to the very point they set out from," and the British "reduced to the use of spade and pick axe for defence."

The War for Independence

His summation was indeed accurate; British strategy was floundering. Sea power in the form of blockading the American ports had never been effective. Territorial war had been equally unsuccessful, and the army was back where it started from in July, 1776. Indeed, the last battle between the main British and American armies had taken place. Now the entrance of France created European, Indian, and West Indian theaters of war to compete with the American theater. Now England had only a choice of risks. To blockade the coast of France or even protect the coast of England would require use of ships needed to convoy supplies and troops to America, to say nothing of those ships needed to hold islands in the West Indies. Termination of the war in America would require recognition of independence, and the King was still adamant against this political concession. In this dilemma the ministry first reverted to a desultory naval war in 1778 and 1779, leaving the army more or less at a standstill, and then resumed a military offensive in the South. Pursuing neither course very vigorously, Britain stumbled down the road to defeat. The war was beyond redemption after Clinton fulfilled his first royal orders.

Clinton was a complex character, and although a logical choice to succeed to the command he was an unfortunate one. His record was uneven: intrepid at Bunker Hill, foolish at Charleston, enterprising up the Hudson but not bold enough, aggressive in retreat at Monmouth. Indeed, he was ablest when acting on the defensive, when limited in what he could do, when not much was expected from him. Neurotically insecure, he was haunted by the hobgoblin of full responsibility. He might plan well, but as the time neared for action his confidence drained away and he sought alternatives to adopt in case his main objective proved too difficult. Morbidly sensitive, he quarreled with his colleagues or suspected them of conspiring against him, cried constantly for reinforcements, and regularly tried to resign. He was, in brief, his own enemy, self-centered but never trusting his own judgment. Aristocratic yet never well to do, rather handsome but not impressive or genial, he it was on whose slight and sloping shoulders a shaky ministry rested its burden of warfare for four years.

RHODE ISLAND FAILURE

The French alliance aroused high hopes in America for united military action, but the first effort produced bitter disappointment.

Clinton had seized Newport back in December, 1776, yet his success had never been exploited by the Howes. The British garrison there was dependent on New York City for food and fuel, and the occupation served only to rob the Americans of a northeastern port. When Washington dispatched Sullivan there from Valley Forge in the spring of 1778 to have a try at throwing out the British, he asked Rhode Island, Massachusetts, and Connecticut for five thousand militia. These states responded fully for this offensive in their midst. In July Washington sent up Nathanael Greene, who knew the area thoroughly, and Lafayette with two brigades. Sullivan had more than seventy-five hundred troops as against Major General Robert Pigot's sixty-seven hundred, and more were coming.

As a token of military co-operation, France dispatched Vice-Admiral the Comte d'Estaing with seventeen ships and four thousand troops aboard. They reached Delaware Bay a few days after Howe's transports had completed the evacuation of Philadelphia. Estaing sailed up to Sandy Hook but could not get his biggest ships—bigger than anything Howe had—over the bar at the mouth of the harbor. Washington suggested he proceed to Rhode Island and support Sullivan. Estaing's energy belied his forty-nine years, but, having been for much of his career an army officer, he was cautious as a fleet commander. Ambitious and intelligent, he was of a stormy disposition and let himself become immersed in details from which he could not be extricated because of his stubbornness.

Sullivan conferred with Estaing on July 29; they planned a joint assault for August 9. In preparation Sullivan seized Butt's Hill on the northern end of the island of Rhode Island, and Estaing began landing troops on a nearby island, when Admiral Howe appeared with more than twenty ships. The Frenchman re-embarked his soldiers and put out to sea for a naval engagement. Sullivan meanwhile approached Newport and began siege operations. The customary Sullivan luck blew in with an unprecedented storm that battered and scattered both squadrons. Estaing limped back in sight on August 20 and declared that according to his instructions Boston was the place for him to refit. Greene assured him that the job could be done right there in Narragansett Bay; Sullivan and Lafayette urged him at least to leave the troops to help with the siege. Estaing assented to this plea, but when the French army officers declined to remain he acceded to their wish. In the face of supplication the French departed. Their conduct so embittered the Americans that three thousand of the militia marched off. Sullivan gave up his siege and fell back to Butt's Hill.

The British now moved out of Newport and stormed the American position on August 29. They were roundly repulsed with heavy loss. In this action a newly raised Rhode Island regiment of Negroes under the adaptable Colonel Christopher

Disappointments in Battle and Alliance

Greene distinguished itself. Sullivan received word that Clinton had sent reinforcements to Newport and therefore gave up his island toe hold the next night. Once more Glover's amphibious regiment ferried the army to the mainland. It was well that Sullivan withdrew, for on the following day Clinton himself arrived with five thousand men.

This example of French assistance antagonized America. In November Estaing left Boston for the West Indies. Was this to be the fruit of foreign alliance? Washington tried to soothe Sullivan's understandable irritation as he realized that military co-operation was going to be strictly according to France's convenience.

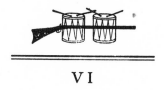

V I

Frontiers in Flames

For more than three years the American colonies had been fighting the enemy in their heartland. There were also frequent clashes on the perimeter—the Atlantic Ocean and the wilderness frontier, long and deep. The early campaign in Canada was one of these. Now, while fighting languished in the central theater, the border warfare west, south, and on the seas flared up in violence.

On orders from London, Clinton reluctantly detached part of his troops southward, and Lieutenant Colonel Archibald Campbell sailed from New York with thirty-five hundred men at the end of November, 1778. He landed in Georgia, between the mouth of the Savannah River and the capital city of Savannah, where he was to be reinforced from British Florida. South of him lay the American general Robert Howe, with seven hundred Continentals and one hundred and fifty militia at Sunbury. In spite of the disparity of numbers, Howe promptly moved up and got between Savannah and Colonel Campbell. He posted himself on the road to block the British advance. Campbell made a frontal assault plus a flank attack from a swamp and broke up Howe's stand. Overwhelmed, the Americans lost 83 killed and 453 taken prisoners. Campbell then moved easily into Savannah, a town of less than thirty-five hundred, and in January, 1779, sent troops more than a hundred miles up the river to occupy Augusta.

In the fall of 1778 Washington had sent Major General Benjamin Lincoln to South Carolina to command the new Southern Department. Upon Campbell's approach Lincoln had moved down toward the Savannah River, where he was joined by the remnants of Howe's defeated army. On paper he had thirty-six hundred men, but actually only twenty-four hundred fit for duty. Unable to take the offensive, he guarded the border of South Carolina from invasion. Meanwhile, the British gathered strength as many loyalists rallied to the colors and as Brigadier General Augustin Prevost, commander at St. Augustine, Florida, moved up to Savannah with nine hundred men. In February, 1779, he tried to cross the river and invade South Carolina, but Lincoln sent out General Moultrie, who drove Prevost back with small loss. Within the same week, the Americans snatched another small victory. A group of several hundred loyalists from North Carolina tried to pass down through the back country to join the British in Georgia. Brigadier General Andrew Pickens surprised them at Kettle Creek, far up the Savannah, killed more than forty, wounded many, and captured seventy. Emboldened, Lincoln sent Brigadier General John Ashe toward Augusta, but he was routed at Briar Creek on March 3 with heavy loss.

The British so maintained their stranglehold on Georgia that the thirteenth colony was taken completely and permanently out of the war, and a loyal government was re-established. Fortunately for the American cause, it was the least populous and most remote of the states. This consideration did not alter the grim fact that the enemy now had an extensive base from which to drive north as well as a fresh reminder of the loyalists available in the South.

Loyalist strength in the region turned the rebel bid for independence into frightful civil war. Since neither side wanted to meet in a major battle, fighting took the form of plundering raids and furious slaughter, as neighbors fell on neighbors. It was marauding without quarter, and both sides committed atrocities. Americans fought each other with greater savagery than the Continentals fought the British. Andrew Jackson as a lad of thirteen participated in the endless skirmishing, lost his two brothers from wounds, and himself was hacked and captured. He never forgot the cruelties his family suffered.

As Lincoln secured more militia, he tried an offensive. Crossing the upper Savannah, he took Augusta in April, 1779. Prevost countered this stroke by jumping the river and taking Purrysburg, South Carolina. His success led him to advance on Charleston, pushing Moultrie back before him. This invasion forced Lincoln to hurry back from the west to defend Charleston. His timely arrival closed the door in Prevost's face. The British encamped on James Island, south of the city, and fortified Stono Ferry. Prevost then returned to Savannah by sea, leaving nine hundred men under Lieutenant Colonel John Maitland. Lincoln sent twelve hundred men under Moultrie to attack him in June, but the solid fortifications and obstinate defense kept the Americans at bay. Moultrie showed up poorly in an action that cost 146 Americans killed and wounded and 155 missing, probably deserted. Yet Maitland soon evacuated the place and retired to Port Royal Island, halfway back to Savannah. Prevost's thrust had gained him nothing but enormous plunder from the plantations and about three thousand slaves, many of whom were sold later to the West Indies.

KENTUCKY AND THE WEST

Before 1775 westward-looking Americans had pushed to the Ohio River at Wheeling (West Virginia), while others had gone on to Kentucky by the river or overland through the Cumberland Gap. Settlements, or stations, had been made at Harrodsburg, Boonesborough, and a few other clearings by 1778. Both the Cherokees and Shawnees claimed this "dark and bloody ground," and scalping parties raided regularly. By the same year, settlements had arisen in northeastern Tennessee on the Holston, Watauga, and Nolichucky rivers, with one lone station on the Cumberland in the vicinity of modern Nashville.

The vast interior was enemy territory in the sense that it was spotted with British posts, and the Indians for the most part were their allies. Garrison troops were maintained along the rim at Forts Niagara, Detroit, and Mackinaw City, then down at Kaskaskia in Illinois, Manchac on the lower Mississippi, Mobile, and Pensacola. Vincennes, on the Wabash, and the Illinois settlements on the middle Mississippi were inhabited by Frenchmen who grudgingly had given allegiance to George III since 1763. New Orleans had been in Spanish hands since 1766, and St. Louis was a struggling trading post in Spanish territory almost beyond the reach of law.

As for the Indians, they easily turned hostile toward the Americans who were intruders on their hunting grounds. In the South the Cherokees had taken up the hatchet in 1776 and harassed the frontier of the Carolinas, only to draw down on themselves militia forces that scorched their villages. The

Creeks tried to remain neutral, and the Catawbas rather favored the Americans. Farther north the Delawares and Shawnees disliked the growing traffic on the Ohio, while the Great Lakes tribes and the Illinois confederation simply waited for British leadership before sweeping down on Kentucky. The powerful Iroquois of western New York were completely at the call of the British Indian agents. So far, the Indians had fought principally by sending war parties east to augment the redcoats, as in St. Leger's expedition in 1777.

An offensive in the West was initiated by Lord Germain. Through Governor Carleton he ordered Henry Hamilton, lieutenant-governor of Detroit, to organize raiding parties of Indians under white leaders and "employ them in making a Diversion and exciting an alarm upon the frontiers of Virginia and Pennsylvania." Kentucky was included as a county of Virginia. This instruction reached Colonel Hamilton in June, 1777, after Carleton had already called for warriors to aid Burgoyne. Consequently, the first big raid on Kentucky waited until February, 1778, when Daniel Boone was captured and carried in triumph to Detroit. Later he escaped. Americans were quick to recognize Detroit as the headquarters of hostility and urged an expedition against it. Two abortive attempts from Pittsburgh in 1778 resulted only in the resignation of the post commanders.

Meanwhile a young Kentucky settler, a tall surveyor with red hair, developed his own idea of a proper offensive. George Rogers Clark believed that the Indian raids on Kentucky could be lessened by overturning British authority in the Illinois country and at Vincennes, then rolling with the momentum to Detroit from the southwest. He saw the French as potential allies. Clark hiked to Williamsburg in the fall of 1777 to see

Frontiers in Flames

Governor Patrick Henry and argue Virginia's responsibility for protecting her new county in the West. The governor and his advisers liked Clark's plan, and although he was only twenty-five years old they persuaded the Virginia Assembly to authorize his expedition without disclosing its destination. Clark hurried up to Pittsburgh and enlisted men to "defend Kentucky." He also sent to Tennessee for help. The frontiersmen, not more than 200 and only half what Clark expected, gathered on an island opposite the site of modern Louisville in May, 1778. When he told the men of their destination, several deserted, but he embarked down the river late in June with 175 adventurous souls. He had the kind of personality that convinced men his goals were attainable. If he was not quite a military genius, he remains one of those remarkable and unaccountable products of the frontier.

Clark did not follow the Ohio to the Mississippi, but struck off across southern Illinois to approach the French settlements from the "back" by surprise. His troops came in sight of Kaskaskia at dusk on July 4 and easily took possession of the town from the handful of British soldiers. A detachment moved on to Cahokia and quickly received its submission. Clark won over the habitants by his secret weapon—news of the French alliance—and they were eager to advise their friends in Vincennes to join in the new allegiance. Father Pierre Gibault and Dr. Jean Laffont set off for the Wabash town with a proclamation from Clark and letters from the populace. Assured that their property would not be taken or their persons molested or moved, the people of Vincennes readily became "Virginians" on July 20.

Then Clark turned his attention to the neighboring Indians. Reversing the traditional policy of soliciting friendship, he voiced no entreaty, passed out no presents. Instead he bruskly told the assembled chiefs that he was a fighting man, that they could have war or peace, and that he cared not in the slightest which they chose. This bold stand won their respect, and if they did not immediately declare for peace they gave signs of loosening their bonds with the Detroit British.

As soon as Colonel Hamilton heard of Clark's success, he formed an expedition to re-establish British authority. Adding 130 French militia and 70 Indians to a detachment of 35 regulars, he started down the Detroit River early in October, 1778. From Lake Erie in forty or more boats, the mixed troop ascended the Maumee River to modern Fort Wayne, Indiana, portaged to the Wabash, and descended on Vincennes December 17. Clark had sent only four men to direct affairs at Vincennes, and Captain Leonard Helm had no choice but to surrender. The fickle Vincennese quickly renewed their oath to the King. Hamilton then made his mistake of deciding to remain in Vincennes for the winter; in consequence his Indians took their leave and over half his militia were permitted to return home. To compound his error, he alienated the local French by failing to conceal his British contempt for them as a people. His only positive action was to rebuild the fort and name it Fort Sackville—for the family name of Lord Germain.

When Clark learned of Hamilton's arrival in Vincennes, he determined to take the offensive at once. He had let some of his men go back to Kentucky, but he enlisted 172, half of them French volunteers, and started out February 6, 1779, on a march of 180 miles. "Great things," he wrote optimistically to Governor Henry, "have been effected by a few men well conducted." An early thaw had caused creeks to flood the prairie until the whole way seemed to lie through swamps. The men suffered keenly from cold, wet, and skimpy provisions for seventeen days. On reaching Vincennes, Clark sent word for the habitants to stay in their houses. He began the attack on the fort at night, when his sparse force could not be counted. The frontiersmen were better marksmen than the British and added credence to the report Hamilton received that Clark had brought five hundred men. The Detroit militia already stood somewhat in awe of the red-haired fighter, and when Hamilton received a demand for surrender next morning they exhibited a reluctance to continue fighting their Illinois relations. Nevertheless, Hamilton refused, with a pompous reference to such conduct as "unbecoming the character of British Subjects."

At this juncture a party of Hamilton's Indians who had been scouting toward the Ohio returned to town innocent of the battle. Clark's men turned and fired on them, killing one, wounding two, and capturing five. Then in full view of the fort four of the captives were tomahawked. Hamilton sent out Captain Helm to tell Clark he would talk terms.

Hamilton surrendered a garrison of 79 men. Clark released the French militia but sent Hamilton and the regulars to Virginia as prisoners, where they languished in the jail at Williamsburg. Clark returned to Kaskaskia, as he expected a big reinforcement from Virginia that would enable him to march on Detroit. Only 150 men reached him, and reluctantly he gave up the enterprise. The American offensive in the West deteriorated to occasional raids on Ohio Indian villages. Nevertheless, Clark's exploit was a shining achievement. His march across flooded Illinois may not compare for hardship with Arnold's long journey through the Maine wilderness in 1775, yet the issue was happier, the victory complete and significant. British power in the West was broken, and, despite the failure to take Detroit, Clark helped make it possible for the vast area to be included within the boundaries of the United States of America at the peace treaty.

Active loyalists kept the New York frontier in flames after the rebuff of St. Leger's expedition in 1777. They were aided by the Iroquois, who had long been tied to British interest. Fort Niagara was the headquarters for raiding parties, red and white. Most deeply involved were the Butlers, father and son: Major John Butler, who had served with St. Leger and since then had raised a battalion of loyalist Rangers, and Captain Walter Butler, former law student who had been captured from St. Leger's army but had escaped confinement in April, 1778. The two officers, instigated by the British, planned to lead a detachment of 110 Rangers and nearly 500 Indians against the settlement in the Wyoming Valley on the upper Susquehanna River in northern Pennsylvania. This region had been in dispute between Connecticut and Pennsylvania owing to the old charter claims of the former, and settlers from the two colonies had clashed in bloody strife three times before the Revolution. Most of them became rebels, but a few were loyalists.

Forty Fort, near modern Wilkes-Barre, was the chief defensive work in the valley, and to it some three hundred rebels and their families fled on the approach of the dreaded Butlers and their Indians. When the marauders began burning and pillaging the outlying houses, the American militia under Colonels Zebulon Butler and Nathan Denison foolishly issued from the fort to give battle. Outnumbered, they were beaten and fled. Colonel Denison took about sixty men back into the fort to protect the women and children there. He capitulated on July 4, and none of the people was injured. However, the soldiers who had fallen wounded were butchered, and those who had fled were hunted down and killed. With the remaining loyalists in the valley, the Butlers retired to Niagara after this bloody foray. In telling of the raid Americans made their names anathemas on the frontier.

Farther north, in New York State, the inhabitants of Cherry Valley freely predicted that they would be the next victims. It was clear that the Butlers would strike again; roving bands of loyalists were growing more insolent, and Joseph Brant, the Anglophile Mohawk leader, had been scouting the vicinity. New York stationed some troops there. Washington had wisely but painfully declared that, since he had the main enemy army to face, protection of the frontier must be a state problem. Fort Schuyler still held, a vexing salient to the British. Unable to take it, their tactic was to swing around the fort and strike at small settlements behind it. Bitter, misguided men, many of the loyalists who enrolled as Rangers owned property they had abandoned or were separated from wives and children held by the rebels for their good behavior.

In September, 1778, they struck at the German Flats and melted away. In retaliation, the rebels burned some Indian villages in October. Captain Walter Butler then brought 200 Rangers to Chemung (Chemung, N.Y.), a Seneca village, on his way to Cherry Valley. A little farther on his way he met Brant with 442 Indians who grudgingly joined Butler, although the chief outranked him. In a cold rain on November 11 this mixed force swept down on the valley settlement of some forty houses. A fort in the town held 250 regulars under Colonel Ichabod Alden. As the garrison this time did not venture out,

Butler and Brant burned the houses, slaughtered 31 or 32 civilians, and took 47 others as prisoners. When Colonel Alden took out a reconnaissance party, he was caught and killed along with 8 of his soldiers. That night Brant demanded that the prisoners be turned over to his Indians for torture, but Butler refused, sending 38 into the fort and keeping the others to exchange for loyalist families. Butler's humane gesture by no means wiped the stain from his name, nor did it halt the excesses of the loyalists in making the states where they had lived untenable for themselves in the future.

SULLIVAN'S EXPEDITION

The Cherry Valley raid, like the earlier ones, provoked retaliation, and the New York frontier flamed again and again. Appeals for a powerful punitive force to carry a torch into the Iroquois country were made to Congress, and early in 1779 that body authorized Washington to take effective steps to safeguard the frontier and to chastise the Indians. After consulting several frontier officers, Washington determined to detach General Sullivan on this mission with three brigades under William Maxwell, Enoch Poor, and Edward Hand—a total of nearly three thousand men including an artillery regiment with small cannon. In addition, a fourth brigade of twelve hundred under James Clinton would join him on the march.

Washington's instructions to Sullivan were brief and inclusive: total devastation of the Iroquois settlements and capture of as many prisoners as possible for hostages; if any warriors sued for peace, they should attack Fort Niagara as a condition of friendship. The three brigades rendezvoused at Easton, Pennsylvania, in May, 1779, and began cutting a road northwestward to the Wyoming Valley. Sullivan was delayed by tardy and insufficient supplies, but in July the expedition moved up to Tioga (Athens, Penn.), near the point where the Chemung or Tioga River from the northwest joins the Susquehanna. The Iroquois, gathering to stop the Americans, made darting raids on settlements in a vain effort to divide Sullivan's force.

Clinton, a New York general, first took his brigade up the Mohawk River, then turned down to Lake Otsego, the head of the Susquehanna. Marching, and floating his supplies, he destroyed fourteen Indian towns on the way down to Tioga. On August 22 he reached the fort that Sullivan had built and placed himself under the latter's command. The enlarged expedition turned up the Chemung River toward a considerable Indian village called Newtown (near Elmira, N.Y.). There the savages, with loyalist help, decided to make a stand against this juggernaut.

Both Butlers, Sir John Johnson, their rival for British favor, and about two hundred Rangers had joined Joseph Brant and more than a thousand warriors. Under white direction breastworks were thrown up. When Sullivan came upon the prepared ground August 29, he deployed his troops and made a frontal attack. With his cannon, riflemen, and superior numbers, he rolled over the position, sent the enemy scattering, and poured into the town with the loss of only eight killed and thirty-five wounded. There the army rested, burning the huts and nearby fields of corn.

When the march was resumed another abandoned village was found and burned. Then the army swung directly north to Catherine's Town at the head of Seneca Lake. After reducing it to ashes, the expedition pushed up the west side of the lake, turned west past the outlet of Canandaigua Lake, and went as far as the great Seneca town of Geneseo. It was beautiful country in the early fall, fruitful with corn, beans, squash, melons, and orchards, but Sullivan was compelled to lay it waste. The Butlers made a second, weak stand, capturing a reconnoitering party sent out by Sullivan and subjecting poor Lieutenant Thomas Boyd and his sergeant to indescribable torture. Geneseo, or Little Beard's Town, on the Genesee River (near Cuylerville) consisted of 128 houses and extensive gardens. Approximately fifty miles from the Niagara River, it was the end of the line for Sullivan. After flattening the town with torches, he retraced his steps, sending farther eastward a detachment that circled Cayuga Lake. The whole army returned to Tioga on September 30 and then marched to Easton. It rejoined Washington's main body early in November.

Sullivan and Clinton together had destroyed forty-one Indian towns, defeated them in one pitched battle, and lost only forty-one men. If they had failed to capture any Indians or to reduce them to suing for peace, they had broken their power for the time being. Their towns and fields devastated, the Iroquois were thrown on the British for support, and many of them starved to death during the winter. Perhaps it was all that could be expected from a sweep that could not entrap such a mobile enemy. Sullivan had been ill on the expedition and on November 30 resigned his commission. Washington was sorry, as he had always held a good opinion of this fighting Irishman and staunch friend. Sullivan was promptly elected to Congress from New Hampshire and, whatever the true state of his health then, lived fifteen years longer.

In a companion move farther west, Colonel Daniel Brodhead, commandant at Pittsburgh and an ambitious martinet popular with no one, had gathered six hundred men in August and marched northward up the Allegheny River. As a whiplash to

Sullivan's main stroke, he terrorized the Munsees and Senecas of northwestern Pennsylvania by burning their towns as they fled before him. It was a small exploit, well executed. He covered four hundred miles in a month, and his resoluteness persuaded the Delawares of Ohio to make peace with him.

THE LOWER MISSISSIPPI

Clark's success in Illinois and at Vincennes, Sullivan's campaign, and Brodhead's marked the high tide of American fortunes on the frontier, but the British would not stay subdued. They even planned an ambitious offensive in the West for 1780. Forces from Florida and Michigan were to march toward each other on the Mississippi, then turn up the Ohio together toward the Appalachians. Laudable as their courage was, they had waited too long.

Spain had come in to the war in May, 1779, but only after driving a hard bargain with Vergennes, who overestimated Spain's help. France agreed to aid Spain in the recovery of Gibraltar, Minorca, the Bay of Honduras, and Florida. Although Spain was not a member of the Franco-American alliance, the United States found herself committed through France to remain at war until Gibraltar had been won for Spain. The deal did not endear France to America, and Spain was not welcomed as a prospective southern neighbor.

Nevertheless, the Americans found a fighter in Bernardo de Gálvez, twenty-three-year-old governor of New Orleans, who moved with energy unusual in a Spaniard. He had already sold powder, loaned money, and opened his port to the United States. He seized the British posts of Manchac, Baton Rouge, and Natchez in September, 1779. Then boldly he turned on Mobile and captured it in March, 1780, leaving only Pensacola and St. Augustine still flying the British flag. This precipitate step ruined the British western scheme. The English at Fort Mackinac sent a force against St. Louis and the Illinois country that was rebuffed by local resistance. Detroit launched Captain Henry Bird with more than a thousand Indians against Kentucky in April, 1780. After a quarrelsome delay they attacked two settlements in June and carried off 350 prisoners (some of them neutralists) before the savages were frightened away by Clark's approach.

These two setbacks emphasized that British authority in the West faced a more subtle defeat: every season thousands more Americans poured down the western slopes of the Alleghenies and up through the Cumberland Gap. It has been estimated that twenty thousand people flowed into Kentucky in 1779—after Hamilton's capture and well before Bird's expedition was planned. What could Detroit avail against that? Although some of the arrivals undoubtedly had sought to escape military service and a few were loyalist in sympathy, the potential increase in American militia was overwhelming. The British might make darting raids but could do little more than cling to the watery rim of the Northwest. In the South their hold on Florida was tenuous.

VII

The War on the Sea

Along the eastern frontier—the Atlantic—the young and small American navy was reaching its effective peak by 1779. It had been organized in the fall of 1775 when Congress formed a Naval (later Marine) Committee which promptly purchased four merchant vessels and armed them. Each state was allowed to create a navy and direct its operation, a necessary authorization, perhaps, but ruinous to a Continental navy. In other legislation Congress established a marine corps so as to have fighting troops aboard the ships, and set up rules to govern prizes taken. John Adams drew up most of this legislation, basing it on English law and practice.

It was obvious from the beginning that the greatest damage to British shipping was going to be inflicted by privateers—privately owned ships equipped with a few cannon and authorized by letters of marque, issued by the state governments or by the Congress, to prey on enemy commerce without being considered pirates. The reward to such shipowners and to their masters and crews was sale of the vessels they captured (prizes) and brought into port. Congress decreed that privateers could keep and distribute all the money derived from merchantmen taken. Naval vessels commissioned by Congress or the states could retain two-thirds of the value of a captured transport or supply ship and one-half that of a warship, the remainder going to the government.

Besides the four ships purchased, Congress ordered in December, 1775, thirteen frigates to be built and in January bought four more merchantmen to convert. The competition for crews became not only spirited but desperate and discouraging. Of the three kinds of service open to seamen, the vast majority preferred to sign aboard privateers, where the risk was no greater but the chance of gaining a small fortune was so much larger. Privateering thus throttled development of a navy. Navy ships often sailed shorthanded, or with green crews, or hired foreigners, or even with English prisoners who could be made to serve.

The Continental navy eventually put fifty to sixty ships in service, although not all at one time. Nothing bigger than a frigate capable of carrying thirty-two guns was built at first, but France sold or loaned to the United States an occasional ship with more guns. The several state navies added another forty or so ships. Together these naval vessels sank or captured nearly two hundred royal ships. In contrast, the British navy in 1775 had 270 ships (131 carrying sixty guns or more) and increased the number to 468 in 1783 (174 with sixty cannon or more). On the other hand, more than two thousand American vessels were employed in privateering. They accounted for the loss of some six hundred enemy ships by the end of the war.

Congress gave command of its burgeoning fleet to Commo-

The War on the Sea

dore Esek Hopkins, an old salt from Providence and brother of a Naval Committee member. Captains of the first four ships were Dudley Saltonstall, Abraham Whipple, Nicholas Biddle, and John B. Hopkins, son of the commodore. These were not auspicious choices. The commodore was dismissed at the end of 1777 for his excessive caution. Saltonstall was fired the same year after the fiasco of the Penobscot expedition, and young Hopkins was suspended at that time and served no more. The ablest captain, Biddle, was killed in battle in the spring of 1778. Only Whipple distinguished himself by lasting until 1780, when he surrendered to the British.

It remained for the senior lieutenant appointed by Congress to display the seamanship and fighting qualities that approached naval genius. He was a Scotsman named John Paul, born in 1747, who had left his homeland at twelve to go to sea. After killing a mutinous sailor in 1773, he added Jones as a protective surname and was visiting his brother in Virginia when war broke out. He was promoted to captain early in 1776 and fought for five years before getting any pay. Tagged by bad luck, strangely indifferent to prize money, a stern disciplinarian, and unpopular with his crews, Jones understood the purposes of a navy, and as a stubborn fighter he gave the United States navy a glorious tradition from its start.

Naval action began with a small coup when Esek Hopkins took eight ships in the spring of 1776 and descended on Nassau in the Bahamas. With two hundred marines he captured the fort and the governor and carried off powder, cannon, and other stores. The little fleet could do nothing against Admiral Howe's great armada that arrived in New York in July, 1776. Activity was confined to taking prizes up and down the coast and in the West Indies.

The War for Independence

When Jones took command of a new eighteen-gun ship the "Ranger" in 1777, he raised the first Stars and Stripes to be used by the navy. He set out for France and arrived with the news of Burgoyne's surrender. France had allowed her ports to be used for the repair of American vessels, and ships taken as prizes were sold there. The British ambassador always protested, and Foreign Minister Vergennes always replied that he would do something about it. He had in fact just closed the ports, but opened them again after Burgoyne's defeat. Benjamin Franklin found Jones a fighting man after his own heart and set about getting him more and better equipment.

Yet at the end of 1777 the naval picture was not bright. American hopes had not been realized. Only four of the thirteen frigates ordered two years before were at sea. Of the rest of the fleet, one ship had been captured, one lost, two were destroyed to prevent their falling into the hands of the enemy, two more were soon to be burned, and three were blockaded in ports. Britain held easy command of the seas by having a hundred vessels in American waters. Still, United States ships had taken 464 enemy merchantmen, of which 72 were recaptured. The British possibly may have seized an equal number of American carriers, but they were mostly smaller ships used in coastwise trade.

The year 1778 began a little better with a second American raid on Nassau that netted powder and five ships. Three ships blockaded in port escaped to sea. From France Jones sailed in the "Ranger" up toward Scotland in April and struck at the border port of Whitehaven. His men rowed ashore, spiked the guns in the fort, then set fire to some vessels at the dock. Crossing to St. Mary's Isle, he intended to kidnap the Earl of Selkirk as hostage for better treatment of American seamen in

British hands. The earl was absent, and Jones let his men steal silver plate from the mansion. Afterward he bought the plunder from his crew and returned it to Lord Selkirk. Outside an Irish harbor he captured a ship. England had been nervously anticipating an invasion fom France, but she certainly did not expect raids by American arms! Jones's foray provoked a storm of reaction all out of proportion to its importance. He was branded a pirate, ports were strengthened, invasion fears mounted, and the remote war in the colonies suddenly came home to the British people.

With the signing of the French alliance, a squadron under the Comte d'Estaing appeared in America with the disappointing results already related. The first battle between France and England had occurred off the coast of France, but the real contest was in the West Indies, to which Estaing repaired. The French seized the British isle of Dominica. France already owned the Santo Domingo portion of Hispaniola and the large islands of Guadeloupe, Martinique, and St. Lucia. However, when Sir Henry Clinton was ordered to dispatch five thousand troops to the West Indies, Rear-Admiral Samuel Barrington was able to retaliate by seizing St. Lucia. Estaing tried to retake it and landed troops, but their assaults were thrown back with heavy casualties, and the island remained in British hands till the end of the war.

The American navy seldom fought as a fleet or disputed coastal waters with the patrolling British ships. It did not interfere with the raid up the New England coast in September, 1778, that destroyed many small ships and storehouses. Our ships hunted the sea lanes for single prizes and did not stand still except statistically: the navy lost nine ships and gained nine by construction or capture.

The War for Independence

Jones returned to France and was ashore a year trying to procure ships from our ally. He was there in February, 1779, when a new frigate, the "Alliance," arrived from America under Captain Pierre Landais, a French naval officer enrolled in the American navy, who had suffered a mutiny on the crossing. The ship brought Lafayette home on a visit. France now gave Jones a clumsy old merchant ship which he had converted into a 42-gun man-of-war and renamed the "Bonhomme Richard" in honor of Franklin's Poor Richard of almanac fame. In June, Jones put out to sea along with the "Alliance" and its petulant commander and three French vessels. Sailing up toward Scotland they took some prizes and, in September off Flamborough Head, met the English "Serapis" of 50 guns and the "Countess of Scarborough" of 20.

With spectacular daring Jones took on both of them. His only defense against the heavier guns of the "Serapis" under Captain Richard Pearson was to move in close and use small arms. His first attempt ran the bow of the "Richard" into the stern of the enemy. Captain Pearson called out: "Has your ship struck?"

"I have not yet begun to fight!" Jones answered, which was true enough.

The ships separated, but again Jones turned across the bow of the "Serapis" in a T formation. Then they swung together side by side, the muzzles of their cannon touching. Jones himself helped lash the two vessels together.

"Well done, my brave lads," he exulted. "We have got her now!"

An unprecedented battle of two hours in the moonlight now began. Pearson's biggest cannon were limited to blowing between decks. Jones's marines took to the rigging to pick off the British gunners and make it too hot for them to stay on deck. Landais came up tardily and fired twice—on the "Richard"! Several sailors were killed, the ship's side was torn open, and she was afire a dozen times. One of the marines saw a hatch partly open and dropped a grenade through it. Down it bounced on a British gun crew, blew twenty of them to bits, and burned others. Jones then concentrated his three light cannon on the mainmast of the "Serapis."

Pearson tried a boarding party, but it was repulsed, and the slugging match resumed. More than a hundred English prisoners on the "Richard" were liberated to man the pumps of the sinking ship. Her life was limited. Then the mainmast of the "Serapis" began to go, and Captain Pearson wavered with it. He pulled down the Red Ensign himself.

The "Richard" was doomed. Jones moved to the damaged "Serapis," repaired her, and took her into Holland. The "Countess of Scarborough" had surrendered to one of his French ships. This was naval warfare that the English had to respect.

Franklin, delegated by the Congressional Marine Committee to manage naval affairs in Europe, promptly fired the erratic Landais. Silas Deane, who constantly opposed Franklin, advised Landais to keep his command. Jones let the malefactor sail to America with the much-needed "Alliance." On the way Landais gave such clear evidence of aberration that he had to be relieved and confined. In the States he was court-martialed and dismissed.

Jones's signal victory was offset by a disastrous expedition from Boston up to Penobscot Bay, Maine. Without consulting Washington, Massachusetts decided to use its state fleet of nineteen ships plus transports to carry nine hundred militia and assault the British-held port. Commodore Saltonstall commanded the ships, and Paul Revere served as chief of artillery. The militia was landed to storm the fort, but for insufficient reasons Saltonstall gave no naval support. He would not attack the three enemy ships in the harbor for fear of the cannon in the fort. When a British squadron arrived on August 13, he put up a weak defense and lost his ships. The defeat not only wiped out the Massachusetts navy but depleted its trading fleet, cost one and three-fourths million pounds sterling, and thirty casualties. It also abruptly ended Saltonstall's career.

The French navy showed up unevenly in 1779. Estaing captured the islands of St. Vincent and Granada in July and then worsted a British fleet that disputed him, but let four of the enemy's disabled ships escape and reduced his sea victory to a draw. Receiving word from Governor John Rutledge of South Carolina of the British hold on Georgia, Estaing responded to the urgent appeal for help and took a considerable fleet of thirty-two ships, plus transports filled with four thousand soldiers, to the mouth of the Savannah River on September 1. He captured four British ships on the way. With him were two captains soon to demonstrate greater ability than their commander. They were the Comte de Grasse, who was to return in two years with a powerful fleet, and Pierre-André de Suffren, who was almost to break England's grip on India.

Estaing landed thirty-five hundred troops below Savannah and was presently joined by General Lincoln from Charleston with fifteen hundred Continentals and militia. The British, under General Augustin Prevost, numbered about twenty-four hundred behind intrenchments, but would have fallen to an

immediate attack by the French. Instead, the allies began pon-
derous siege operations, moving cannon from the ships and
using up three more weeks. Impatient Estaing then decided to
storm a redoubt on October 9. A deserter informed the enemy,
and the reinforced redoubt held off the assault in bitter fighting. The attackers advanced unevenly, never too many for the
British to bring under a withering fire. The allies lost heavily—
172 killed including Count Pulaski and 580 wounded including
Estaing—before they gave up. The siege might have been continued, but Estaing had had enough. He recalled his troops and
sailed away to France. Lincoln marched back to Charleston.
Estaing was criticized again, as he had been at Newport, and
appeared no more in American waters.

Similar uncertainty by Admiral the Comte d'Orvilliers in
France threw away a rare invasion opportunity. When Spain
entered the war in May, 1779, she added thirty-six ships to the
French home fleet of thirty, and the combined armada moved
toward the English channel. On the northern coast of France
fifty thousand troops were poised to invade southern England
as soon as the British fleet was knocked out. To ward off this
approaching doom, the English made small preparation. The
British admiralty was riddled with corruption, from its dissipated first lord, the Earl of Sandwich, down through its place-
seeking admirals, favor-demanding captains, bribe-taking clerks,
and swindling contractors. In the end England was saved by
the inefficiency of the French. After changing his plans,
Orvilliers dallied unreasonably until he suffered a severe storm.
Then he was ordered back to Brest. Another such invasion
force was never assembled, yet England had to keep a large
fleet at home.

The War for Independence

The pervading weakness of the French and Spanish at sea was their uncertain motivation and narrow focus. France had entered the war to humiliate further a struggling England. She did not especially want expensive Canada back, much preferring to increase her empire in the West Indies by capturing islands. Spain wanted the Floridas but coveted more ardently the two places close to home, Gibraltar and Minorca. She had blockaded Gibraltar and expected it to fall like a ripe plum. Britain's deep commitment on the continent of America offered a splendid opportunity to achieve these specific goals. Yet for two hundred years the British navy had built up a reputation for aggressive courage that was a byword in Europe. Neither France nor Spain sought a decisive engagement at sea; indeed, they avoided it, hoping to pick up an island here and there and hold them at the peace table after England, exhausted by the Americans, sued for terms. It was jackal warfare against a wounded lion.

Disappointed in navy performance, Congress dissolved its Marine Committee in the fall of 1779 and replaced it with a Board of Admiralty on which the majority were experts outside Congress. Ships were not being built fast enough, there was no admiral to unify the command, crews were inadequate owing to the lure of privateering, and nothing of great effect was being accomplished. Yet no improvement was forthcoming. Inexplicably, the ablest captain, John Paul Jones, was stranded in France without a ship. Moreover, his recommendations—remarkable papers on the proper role of the navy—were ignored. The navy was not going on to greater achievements. Congress having committed itself, perhaps unavoidably, to a program divided among the Continental navy, state navies,

126

and privateers, the effort at sea was splintered into individual actions. Besides, land warfare exhausted the resources of the young country. For sea power Washington had to look to France. He yearned for superiority along the Atlantic, even for only a few weeks.

Yet the little navy had etched a pattern of limited effectiveness that continued. Armed American ships maintained frequent contact with France. Supplies arrived here regularly; passengers and messages went back and forth safely. Britain never was able to enforce a complete blockade or to cut communications. If our ships were not a grave danger to England, they were an extreme annoyance, costing her money and ships, pinning down squadrons in scattered locations, raising prices of imports to England, and making the war a reality to the British people.

Into the Slough of Despond

Washington's main army, encamped in an arc that crossed the Hudson, conducted no operations for a year, from July, 1778, to July, 1779. Headquarters were maintained at West Point, which served to keep the route open from New England to the South and to prevent the British from pushing northward up the Hudson. The fortifications at the Point were steadily strengthened, and the men continued to drill under Steuben's manual of arms.

The British in New York were no more active. Clinton had moved up to King's Ferry, the most southerly communication across the Hudson, and seized Stony Point and Verplanck's Point, the ferry terminals. His object was to draw Washington down from the highlands into battle, but the American did not rise to the bait. Instead, after the British fortified Stony Point, he called in Anthony Wayne, gave him the new light infantry companies amounting to 1,360 men, and told him to take the place.

This assignment was exactly to Wayne's liking. He reconnoitered the stronghold and provided his colonels with an exact map of the promontory jutting eastward into the river. The corps marched southwestward along secluded trails in the daylight of July 15 and after dark halted west of the fort. Two columns were to climb the rugged slopes on the north and south sides; the third was to march east along a causeway and force the entrance. Only the latter were permitted to load their muskets.

The assault began at midnight. While the British garrison of 680 turned out to resist the attack from the only road into the works, the other light infantrymen scaled the heights and poured onto the plateau with bayonets fixed. Wayne remembered Paoli and did not spare the enemy. The fighting was brief and bloody. The British lost sixty-three killed and seventy-three wounded before the rest surrendered. The victory cost the Americans fifteen killed and eighty-three wounded, the wounded including Wayne, and their effectiveness was a tribute to Steuben's solid training. Wayne wrote to Washington that night: "Our officers & men behaved like men who are determined to be free." A quantity of military stores and equipment was hauled away. The fortifications were destroyed in the next three days, because they would have required a larger number of troops than Washington cared to assign to such a fort.

A month later Major Henry ("Light-Horse Harry") Lee duplicated the feat by surprising Powle's or Paulus Hook, opposite New York, and capturing the garrison. Neither exploit had any tactical value but was more in the nature of a military exercise. They did demonstrate the growing professionalism of the American army, but the lesson was lost on Clinton. Inactive because of delayed reinforcements, he was virtually immobilized by these two blows.

The year brought good news from other localities. The western frontier quieted down after Clark's victories and Sullivan's expedition. The Spaniards had cleared the lower Mississippi of British posts and threatened Mobile and Pensacola. These pressures and others in the West Indies prompted Clinton to abandon Newport, so that New England was at last free of the enemy. To the south the military outlook was dismal. The effort to recover Savannah from the British had failed; and Washington had been disappointed in his hope to see Estaing bring his fleet north for a joint enterprise. When he learned that the admiral had sailed for France, Washington took most of his troops into winter quarters among the hills of Morristown, New Jersey. And it was a winter of confining blizzards and paralyzing cold.

On paper Washington had 27,000 men, but his real strength was much less. The three-year enlistments obtained at the beginning of 1777 were expiring, and by May, 1780, his effectual force was reduced to 10,500. At the same time British strength was building up. By the addition of the Newport garrison and the arrival before winter of Lord Cornwallis with reinforcements from England, Clinton's army was raised to a total of 28,700, of which 10,800 were Germans and 4,000 loyalists, or provincials. It was apparent that the British, disappointed in their navy, would end the long stalemate by opening a land offensive in 1780.

THE HOME FRONT

The American army faced a more insidious enemy, however, than an expanded British force. An economic fact was thrusting itself painfully into every tent and hut: though the colonies might successfully field an army, they were fighting a war they could not pay for. Inflation was paralyzing the military effort while stimulating economic activity among civilians.

War is always costly, and the financial problem facing Congress never was solved. It was postponed until it exploded. The fundamental defect was taxation, that touchy requisite which had provoked rebellious thoughts in the first place. The states could tax themselves and issue their own paper currency, and they did—but in greatly varying proportions. The paper of a few states, being backed by more gold and silver collected in taxes, was more reliable and more avidly sought than the paper of other states which lacked sufficient metal to redeem much of it. On top of all these currencies, Congress issued Continental notes, even though it had no power to tax at all! It could only submit requests to the states for contributions. When not enough responses were obtained to support the central government and the army and navy it was creating, Congress simply printed money anyway and spent it.

The first $20 million put into circulation gave the Revolution a lift, but as emission continued, confidence in the money fell. Merchants who had little faith in this new currency quickly got rid of it by buying more goods (already manufactured items were scarce since English products were cut off) and bidding up prices against other merchants. As retail prices rose, wage-earners demanded higher pay to meet their increased cost of living. Farmers raised the prices on their foodstuffs. There were strikes, and mobs terrorized merchant speculators. Congress, finding that supplies needed by the army cost more, was driven to print more money. Everyone could see the mounting evil of inflation, but no one could brake it.

The War for Independence

Price-fixing and wage-freezing were invoked in 1776 by the New England states meeting in convention. Speculators from other states then poured in, bought up goods at the fixed prices, took them home, and boosted their sale prices to new highs. State embargoes were unenforcible. This drain on the states that tried to stop inflation forced them to abandon controls. As in all wars, a new class of freshly rich began to appear, as peddlers, artisans, contractors, and farm laborers became shopkeepers or produce-merchants. Old fortunes built on foreign trade and big plantations diminished.

Late in 1777 Congress asked the states to levy taxes and to cease issuing notes, both to drain off some of the purchasing power and to strengthen their currency. Massachusetts and Connecticut complied, and a few others acted later, but little was achieved. A decay of morals seemed to accompany the frenzied spending. The military lull created the unfortunate impression that Britain was ready to give up the war. A curious indifference to realities overcame the populace. Everyone was afflicted with the corrupting disease brought on by inflation. Business ethics declined rapidly; "black markets" were organized. Since money was cheap, much was spent on display, and gambling increased furiously. Greater drinking and more frequent dueling seemed to follow. The more thoughtful citizens, observing that the government's weakness permitted inflation and monopoly, began to revise their concept of liberty and to wonder if government should not be the guardian of the many against the ruthless few.

Continental dollar bills depreciated steadily until, at the beginning of 1779, they were worth but twenty-five cents. In this year they plunged rapidly to one cent. "Not worth a Continental" was a bitter expression of lost value. Weakly and mistakenly Congress sought to salvage the situation by declaring that no more than $200 million in notes would be issued. The announcement only pushed prices higher, especially as the quartermaster and commissary departments were spending at the rate of $120 million a year. One way Congress obtained a little money was to draw drafts on France; when they turned up for collection it was Franklin's humiliating duty to plead with Vergennes to honor them.

The situation of the army was not just unhappy but precarious. Washington wrote in April, 1779, that "a waggon load of money will scarcely purchase a waggon load of provision." A captain couldn't buy a pair of shoes with a year's pay. Officers, who had to furnish their own clothes and pay for their food, ran into debt while having nothing to send their families. "I despise my countrymen!" Major Ebenezer Huntington declared in exasperation.

Finally in March, 1780, Congress officially devalued its own currency by decreeing that $40 in paper was worth $1 in gold. By this stroke the national debt was cut from $200 million to $5 million. Not a solution, this repudiation was only an effort to hold the line somewhere on inflation. It also had the effect of making the Revolutionary generation pay most of the cost of the war. Yet prices took another jump, and not only did officers resign in steady numbers, but there were ugly rumors of mutiny among the ranks.

THE SIEGE OF CHARLESTON

Arrival of reinforcements and Lord Germain's nudging for a southern campaign stirred Clinton to undertake an offensive after languishing for eighteen months. The re-establishment of royal authority in Georgia, the sparse population in the Carolinas, the several harbors, the urgings of loyalists in the region (who had not yet experienced life with a British and German army), and the suitable climate for a winter campaign, all had appealed to Germain. Despite the failure of loyalists in New England and the middle colonies to flock to the British colors and take up arms, the old illusion beckoned from the South.

Clinton took with him almost 8,000 troops and Cornwallis as second in command. He had tried again to resign in favor of Cornwallis and therefore expected any week to shift the responsibility to his junior, whom he believed to be Germain's favorite. The prospect only made him more sensitive to any move Cornwallis might seem to make in anticipation of the succession. Moreover, the naval commander of the expedition was Marriot Arbuthnot, an aging and indecisive admiral who had been conspicuously absent from the list of naval officers Clinton had recommended as successors to Lord Howe. Thus the campaign opened with Clinton feeling himself an aggrieved party.

He left New York in the capable hands of Major General von Knyphausen with an army equal to Washington's. The day after Christmas, 1779, the large convoy sailed for Charleston, South Carolina. With its departure the war quietly moved out of the North never to return there in force. It was an unacknowledged confession that loyalism was an ineffective minority voice there, that the flow of independence was a turbulent cataract the British could not dam, and that Washington could not be cornered and defeated.

Germain and Clinton had embarked upon a whole new strategic plan, that of divided forces: one defensive in the North, the other offensive in the South. There was nothing wrong or fatal about such a concept as long as they remembered that it did require control of the coastal sea, since two armies, not one, must be supplied by ship and must be co-ordinated and kept in communication by the navy. But such a strategy, which might have worked in 1776, became much more risky after France and Spain had added their fleets to the enemy's. Whatever thought Clinton may have given to the naval dependence of a divided force, clearly he did not believe the risk a serious one.

The expedition suffered an initial beating from nature on its way south. Violent gales off Cape Hatteras dispersed the fleet (one transport was blown across to England!), damaged the stores, and destroyed most of the horses. The ships converged again off Savannah. There they made repairs and sailed up to Charleston, landing on Johns Island, south of the city, on February 11, 1780. Proceeding orthodoxly but irresistibly, Clinton slowly moved over to James Island, along the Ashley River, to the west side of the city and, at the end of March, crossed the river and stood on the same peninsula as Charleston.

After the British failure late in 1776, South Carolina had allowed its forts on Sullivan's Island and James Island to crumble into ruins. A squadron of nine frigates under Commodore Whipple constituted the coastal protection. Now Governor Rutledge could only build up fortifications on the land side of the town, which he tried frantically to do with slave labor. Washington had detached fifteen hundred Continentals from Virginia and North Carolina to reinforce General Lincoln, who could muster about fifteen hundred other Continentals and twenty-five hundred militia. The long delay in the advance of the British proved to be a deceptive advantage, for with fifty-five hundred troops and the hurried earthworks, Lincoln was led to the fatal decision to defend a position that should have been abandoned. Led or driven, for politically he hardly dared leave the biggest city in the South to its fate without a fight. He kept an escape route northward across the Cooper River guarded by about six hundred infantry and cavalry. As a further safeguard the navy sank four of its ships in the mouth of the Cooper River and pulled the others upstream behind a boom—a move, however, that left the city open to sea approach.

On April 8 a British squadron ran into the lower bay. A week later Clinton began bombarding the town from land batteries across the river and on the Charleston peninsula. As he had left a thousand men in Georgia, he sent back to New York for a reinforcement. There had just arrived at Charleston twenty-five hundred men under Lord Francis Rawdon, an extremely able officer, twenty-five years old, tall and dark, with a curious reputation as the "ugliest man in England." He had fought in America ever since Bunker Hill and now commanded the Volunteers of Ireland, a corps made up of Irish deserters from American units and other loyalists. His addition gave Clinton ninety-five hundred troops, plus five hundred sailors, and Charleston was summoned to surrender.

Lincoln considered the situation desperate and consulted his officers. There was divided opinion, and Lincoln reached no decision. He may have been irresolute; he probably hated to give up at the first demand, especially when he could still retreat. While he temporized, Lieutenant Colonel Banastre Tarleton, aged twenty-six, the dashing, insolent, and peculiarly cruel commander of Clinton's cavalry (now remounted), rode around to the north and on April 14 with Major Patrick Ferguson's corps of marksmen completely routed the troops stationed there. There was no way open for Lincoln now. He considered fighting his way out in order to save part of his army, but the governor's council threatened to turn the townspeople against the army if he moved to leave. He could only endure or surrender. The city held out another month, Lincoln trying but one small sortie.

Clinton developed his approaches methodically, drained the ditch that the slaves had dug, and prepared for a general assault on the fortifications. Again he demanded surrender. Lincoln asked for terms and, upon being refused, ordered a general cannonade. The British replied in kind, and for a day the city endured such a bombardment that the mercurial citizens petitioned Lincoln to give up. On May 12 he capitulated.

It was the biggest victory of the war for the British in numbers captured: six thousand troops, sailors, and armed citizens plus three hundred-odd cannon and five ships—ample revenge for Saratoga. It was the greatest disaster suffered by the Americans in the war, for in addition to the army, Generals Lincoln, Duportail, Moultrie, Scott, Lachlan McIntosh, William Woodford, and James Hogun were lost. Lincoln was criticized for letting himself be cooped up in an indefensible town, but he was unfortunately caught in a painful political situation. Had he saved his army by ruthlessly abandoning the South Carolina capital, the cause might have suffered worse from wholesale defection in the South. Whether he could have achieved by more vigorous sorties anything beyond heavier casualties is questionable. He asked for a court of inquiry on his conduct, but none was ever held.

Resistance in South Carolina seemed to collapse with the fall of Charleston. A regiment of four hundred Virginia Continentals under Colonel Abraham Buford stopped forty miles short of the capital on the day it surrendered and turned back northward. Learning of the force, Tarleton galloped after it, riding 105 miles in 54 hours, some of his horses falling over in the heat. But on May 29 at the Waxhaws, close to the North Carolina border, he overtook Buford. A hasty and poorly arranged defense could not stop the momentum of Tarleton's mounted charge. Buford waved a white flag, and his men called for quarter. But Tarleton let his green-coated legion slaughter at will until there were 113 Virginians killed, 150 wounded, and 53 captured. Less than a hundred escaped the massacre. A new phrase, ominous in its bitterness, swept through the American army: "Tarleton's quarter," a synonym for the butchering of surrendered men, and "Bloody Tarleton" became his name.

Mopping up in South Carolina was comparatively easy. British garrisons were established up the coast at Georgetown, at the mouth of the Pee Dee River; far up the Pee Dee at Cheraw; at Camden, west and south of Cheraw; at Ninety-six, a western post ninety-six miles from the principal Cherokee town; and at Augusta, across the line in Georgia. Clinton issued handbills inviting all the inhabitants to come under the King's protection and renew their allegiance. Measures were taken to restore royal government and bring back the former governor. Yet South Carolina was not quite taken out of the war. Surviving patriots began to gather in remote places and form under partisan leaders—Francis Marion, Andrew Pickens, and Thomas Sumter, men of extraordinary talent for guerrilla warfare. Nevertheless, believing that his conquest presaged a general victory, Clinton sailed for New York on June 8. He left Cornwallis (with whom he had already quarreled) in command, with strict orders to hold South Carolina and to make no move into North Carolina at the risk of losing any of the South

Carolina posts. Cornwallis kept about six thousand troops to garrison Savannah, Charleston, and the minor posts and to provide a mobile field army.

Clinton returned to New York for three reasons. He had received word that a French fleet was expected there, and hence both he and the admiral should return to their main base of operations. Clinton also had formed a plan to fall on Washington's camp at Morristown, acting jointly with Knyphausen. This plan miscarried because on his arrival he found that the German had anticipated him and taken an inadequate force into New Jersey "on the ill-founded suggestions of a certain American Governor and some other over-sanguine refugees." The move accomplished nothing, and Clinton turned his attention to some unfinished business he had left since Christmas: the treason of an American general who called himself Mr. Moore in his correspondence, but clearly was Benedict Arnold.

ARNOLD'S TREASON

Lafayette's year at home in France finally had produced military aid in the form of an army and navy which, to prevent disappointment à la Estaing, was to be placed under Washington's command. With seven ships of the line and five frigates under Admiral Charles d'Arsac de Ternay, transports carrying five thousand troops left France in May and arrived at Newport unmolested on July 11, 1780. Commanding this army was the Comte de Rochambeau, an excellent choice. Polite, free of jealousy and sensitiveness, genuinely admiring of Washington, he spoke no English but utilized the tactful Chevalier de Chastellux as interpreter and intermediary. A veteran of the Seven Years' War, Rochambeau quickly comprehended many of

The War for Independence

Washington's problems and, at fifty-five, had acquired some of his colleague's restraint and dignity.

In enthusiastic anticipation of their arrival, Washington planned a joint descent on New York City. The British, however, moved first and aimed a joint land and sea force at the French in Newport. Washington had to act quickly, as if he were attacking New York alone, in order to force the return of Clinton's troops. The squadron under Arbuthnot proceeded and blockaded the French ships in Narragansett Bay. Washington and Rochambeau conferred at Hartford, Connecticut, in September, and the count insisted that an attack on New York must wait on French naval superiority—that is, until other ships arrived. Disappointed, Washington returned to West Point—to confront heartbreaking treason that narrowly escaped national tragedy.

After a year as military administrator of Philadelphia, Benedict Arnold had deviated from loyal patriotism. Installed as a wounded hero, he immediately revealed a snobbish love of luxury and society, and what had once been the man of action's impatience with financial paper work now became an underhanded zeal to make money by circumventing not merely the proprieties but the law.

His extravagance put him into debt. He formed a secret partnership through which scarce goods might be bought with public credit, sold at a profit, and the proceeds divided after the public money was replaced. He secured an interest in a loaded ship and let it leave Philadelphia, despite Congress' prohibition against moving any property until its owners had been identified. He used army wagons to move some private property in New Jersey, allegedly to save it from British capture. He was given shares in a captured British sloop on his promise to get a larger percentage of the cargo's value awarded to the captors. He sought to get possession of a huge forfeited loyalist estate in New York. Meanwhile, his jumbled public accounts from Quebec and Lake Champlain remained unsettled, and Continental currency skidded down and down. Arnold borrowed heavily from the French consul in Philadelphia and entertained last year's loyalists publicly.

During this time the widower had met and fallen in love with Peggy Shippen, eighteen years old to his thirty-eight years, and married her in April, 1779. She was the daughter of a noted Philadelphia neutralist. Pennsylvania's Executive Council took exception to Arnold's conduct (minor offenses, because they were not aware of the major ones) and published their complaints. On Washington's advice, Arnold asked for a court-martial. To his disappointment the trial was delayed until December, 1779, when he was found guilty of two counts and sentenced to only a reprimand from the commander-in-chief. Washington's letter was a masterpiece of firmness and sympathy.

Experienced yet immature, arrogant and wilful but insecure, generous at times but fundamentally self-centered, Arnold's petulance had already led him to a disastrous step. Early in May, 1779, through a loyalist intermediary, he had offered his services to the British—for money and for preferment when he should join them. To them he professed an abhorrence of separation from England, of Congress' usurpation of authority, and of the French alliance, sentiments he had never voiced earlier.

For the next thirteen months Arnold played his dual role successfully: the maligned American hero who, because of his loyalty to Washington, remained faithful to an ungrateful

Congress, and the sly traitor who transmitted information about Washington and his plans regularly to British headquarters in New York and received pay. His pretty young wife knew of the treason from the beginning. Urged to do something more if he wanted greater rewards, Arnold asked Washington in May, 1780, for the command of West Point. When it was granted and before Arnold moved there, he wrote in code on July 15 to Major John André (who handled Clinton's secret service):

> If I point out a plan of coöperation by which S[ir] H[enry] shall possess himself of West Point, the Garrison, &c. &c. &c. twenty thousand pounds Sterling I think will be a cheap purchase for an object of so much importance.

He also expected to retain his rank in the British army. In case of failure that would force him to go over to the British empty-handed, he wanted £10,000 for the property he would lose and a pension. These bold proposals gave Clinton pause, even though his monarch was then in process of spending £100,000 to get friendly candidates elected to Parliament. West Point was certainly the key to the Hudson, and the garrison might amount to three thousand troops, so £20,000 was perhaps not too high a price. As for the alternative sum merely for Arnold's personal realignment, Clinton implied that he wasn't worth it. After further haggling, it was arranged in September that André should go up the Hudson under a flag of truce and talk with Arnold.

This violation of a flag of truce was rendered fatal by Arnold's first bringing André within the American lines and then sending him back overland in disguise, with incriminating papers hidden in his boot. When he was captured near North Castle, searched, and suspected as a spy, word was naturally

sped to Arnold. This was on September 25, the very day
Washington was expected on his return from the Hartford
conference with Rochambeau. Arnold knew the game was up
for him. Making a brief farewell to his wife, he slipped down
the river in his boat just before Washington's party arrived.
The commander-in-chief found Peggy Arnold in real or well-
feigned hysterics and learned of Arnold's treasonable flight.
Like a problem child who requires special parental handling,
Arnold had secured a special place in Washington's affections
by his weaknesses as well as by his undeniable fighting qualities.
The revelation shook Washington unmercifully. Announce-
ment of the treason was made throughout the army, officers
speaking in suppressed and awful voices, the men stunned and
shaking their heads.

But war would not wait. Washington had lost a general and
in his place had a spy on his hands who by the laws of warfare
deserved to be executed immediately. Yet Washington moved
deliberately, convening a board of officers to consider André's
case. Clinton made strenuous efforts to save his favorite aide
but rejected the one remedy that was unofficially suggested to
him: to trade Arnold for André. The Americans regretfully
hanged the personable young major on October 2.

After trying to collect the £10,000 he had originally asked
for instead of the £6,000 he had been promised by André at
their interview, Arnold sent to Germain a long statement about
the condition of the Continental army. How little he comprehended Washington is revealed by his absurd suggestion that
Britain offer him a title. Arnold also issued a proclamation
calling for other Americans to join him in ending the war. In
spite of worthless paper money, unpaid wages, insufficient
clothes and rations, and general discouragement; against British

promises of food, pay, and plenty of land as a bonus, exactly twenty-eight men deserted to the American Legion Arnold was forming. The British had made a bad bargain all around; one officer commented that Arnold was "to raise a regiment of as great scoundrels as himself, if he can find them."

Arnold's defection had the shock effect of strengthening rather than weakening American morale. This was the more astonishing because it followed abruptly on the receipt of news from the South of a fresh disaster there.

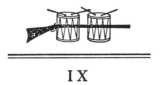

IX

Recovery of the South

After General Lincoln's capture at Charleston, Washington wanted to restore Quartermaster General Nathanael Greene to a field command by putting him in charge of the Southern Department, but Congress gave the post to Horatio Gates, then at his farm in Virginia. Gates moved down to central North Carolina where Baron de Kalb held about a thousand Maryland and Delaware Continentals and Pulaski's surviving cavalry under Colonel Charles Armand-Tufin, all suffering from lack of provisions. North Carolina was sending food to its militia under General Caswell but looked upon the Continentals almost as foreigners.

Gates joined his force to Caswell's in order to get rations and acquired some raw militia from Virginia. On August 14, 1780, he counted forty-one hundred troops on paper, of which three thousand were present fit for duty. He was now down at Rugeley's Mills, South Carolina, thirteen miles north of Camden, a British post commanded by Lord Rawdon with a garrison of thirteen hundred. However, hearing of Gates's approach, Cornwallis had hurried up from Charleston with nine hundred reinforcements to assume command.

Gates prepared for a surprise attack. The men rested on August 15 and were issued some meat, corn meal, and molasses (in the absence of rum). They were ordered to begin a night march at 10 o'clock, and the purgative effect of their diet now struck them. Gates's plan was opposed by his officers because two-thirds of the men were militia who could not keep together or perform maneuvers in the dark, but Gates was determined when he should have reconsidered. His experience with militia at Saratoga let him overestimate them.

By one of those strange coincidences of war, Cornwallis ordered a night march against Gates, also to start at ten o'clock. Without any warning, the two forces collided on the road after midnight and recoiled, waiting for daylight. Kalb was for retreating, but Gates decided to fight it out. He put the militia on the left and the Continentals on the right under Kalb. Again by chance Cornwallis put his regulars on the right, opposite the American militia, and his loyalists plus some regulars on the left under Rawdon.

Gates opened the battle with the last orders he was to issue in the war. The British regulars soon swarmed over the militia and put them to flight. In the smoke and dust, Kalb did not know of this defection and was elated by driving back the British left. Twice more Rawdon rallied his men to attack, only to be beaten off by the valiant men from Maryland and Delaware. Kalb lost his horse and suffered a head wound, but the giant was everywhere, swinging his sword in hand-to-hand action. No orders came from Gates to retreat—for the very good reason that he was no longer in the vicinity. Cornwallis finally had to turn his full force on the six hundred Continentals before Kalb went down with eleven wounds. His troops amazingly charged again, then broke and scattered. The defeat was so complete that no record of casualties remains. At least 750 were killed or captured. The British lost 68 killed and 245 wounded.

Mounted on a noted racer, Gates rode all the way to Charlotte, North Carolina, a distance of 65 miles, that day. His reputation gained at Saratoga was ruined. He hurried on to Hillsboro, 120 miles farther, and there stragglers and fugitives came in to the number of seven hundred—all that remained of the southern army. Dan Morgan forgot the resentment that had prompted him to resign the year before and hurried down from Virginia to join Gates.

Warfare in the South reverted to guerrilla raids by the steadfast partisan leaders, much of the fighting being bloody civil war between small bands of rebels and loyalists, each avenging itself frightfully on the other. Sumter's little force was wiped out, however, on August 18 when Tarleton fell on his camp, killing 150 and capturing 300.

KINGS MOUNTAIN

Cornwallis' success now proved to be his undoing. With South Carolina so thoroughly prostrated, North Carolina became irresistible. Cornwallis believed that conquest of the second province would be easy and would secure the first. He had asked Clinton to send a detachment from New York into Virginia as a diversion and, anticipating compliance, he left Camden on September 7 to march north toward Charlotte. To extend his sweep he ordered Major Patrick Ferguson, who commanded at Fort Ninety-six in the west, to march his loyalists northward also. They were expected to draw others into their ranks and eventually join Cornwallis at Charlotte.

Ferguson was the British answer to Dan Morgan. A professional officer since the age of fifteen, he was now thirty-six and the inventor of a breech-loading rifle that used a pointed bullet and could be fired five or six times a minute. (General Howe had rejected it and put the available rifles in storage.) Ferguson's plundering and burning of rebel homes in western South Carolina had made him the object of particular abhorrence, however. As he tramped up into North Carolina, the mountain settlers, hardy frontiersmen equipped with rifles, gathered to stop him. They emerged on horseback from the hill country where North Carolina, Tennessee, and Virginia meet, and they were tough, purposeful, and deadly efficient. Ferguson smelled trouble and turned back south. They stalked him. Seeing he could not escape a fight, he turned aside to Kings Mountain and put his thousand men on top of this long narrow summit, a position of great natural strength.

On October 7, nine hundred backwoodsmen under Colonels John Sevier and Isaac Shelby of modern Tennessee, William Campbell of Virginia, and Benjamin Cleveland, Charles McDowell, and James Williams of North Carolina rode up for a look. They tied their horses and surrounded the mountain. Then at a signal they began climbing the rugged bluff, firing from tree to tree. Ferguson kept his men moving from spot to spot to repulse the invaders with bullets or bayonets. But Sevier's men reached the top, and when Ferguson's turned on them others swarmed onto the level summit. Formations were impossible and pointless; every man fought for himself. Desperately Ferguson cut down two white flags; then seven rifle bullets tumbled him from his saddle. Some of the terrorized loyalists cried for quarter, but, remembering Tarleton, the frontiersmen yelled "Tarleton's quarter!" and fired on the knots of defenders. It was a gory battle of revenge, and the officers stopped the slaughter with difficulty. Of the loyalists 225 were killed, 163 badly wounded, and 716 taken prisoner. The Americans lost 28 killed and 62 wounded. Some of the prisoners were tried by torchlight for treason, and nine of them were hanged in further retaliation. Most of the over-mountain men, having accomplished what they set out to do, went home again.

Cornwallis was panicked by the news. He left Charlotte and hurried back south to Winnsboro, South Carolina, which lay between Camden and Ninety-six.

Congress recalled Gates from his command and this time directed Washington to name a successor. He immediately appointed Greene and gave him command over all troops from Delaware to Georgia. Greene had won no battles so far, and he was not to win any decisively in the future; yet he had learned how to conduct himself under pressure. He practiced Washington's type of prudence, and he had the temperament for dealing not only with discouragement but also with partisan leaders, contractors, governors, and assemblies. No one then thought he could defeat Cornwallis, but he was to show his lordship a war of maneuver that the latter never could comprehend. Even the historian of the British army ruefully admits that Cornwallis was no match for him.[1]

Knowing how scarce and important supplies were, Greene proceeded southward in deliberate fashion. He got the promise of support from Washington, picked up fifteen hundred mus-

[1] J. W. Fortescue, *A History of the British Army* (London, 1902), III, 403.

kets and some wagons in Philadelphia, pleaded in Delaware for reinforcements, left a supply officer in Baltimore, called on Governor Thomas Jefferson in Virginia for clothing, posted Steuben in Richmond to scrape up anything he could find, and on December 2, 1780, met Gates at Charlotte and relieved him. His "army" then consisted of fifteen hundred infantry, ninety cavalrymen, and sixty artillerists. Half the force was properly equipped, and there were just three days' provisions on hand. "The appearance of the troops was wretched beyond description," he reported.

In desperation to obtain food, Greene divided his army. It was an audacious and seemingly foolhardy move. He gave Dan Morgan 320 Continentals, 200 Virginia riflemen, and Lieutenant Colonel William Washington's cavalry troop, 600 all told, and sent him off southwestward. The remaining troops, numbering more than one thousand, mainly militia, were intrusted to General Isaac Huger of South Carolina, and Greene remained with him. This division moved southeastward to Cheraw. Situated between the two wings, Cornwallis was somewhat puzzled as to which one to pursue. He now had four thousand men at Winnsboro, having ordered the detachment Clinton sent to Virginia under Major General Alexander Leslie to sail on down to Charleston for his reinforcement. Greene, too, got help. Washington sent Light-Horse Harry Lee's Legion, 280 strong; they were not only fully uniformed but a thoroughly disciplined troop of scouts and raiders. Some Virginia militia appeared, and other North Carolina militia joined Morgan, bringing the American total up to twenty-seven hundred effectives.

Clinton had been disappointed by Cornwallis' draft of Leslie's detachment from Virginia, where he wished to establish a base of operations, but he acquiesced. To accomplish his end, Clinton ordered Benedict Arnold to Virginia late in December, 1780, with sixteen hundred troops to find a proper station.

Autumn's inaction in the Carolinas came to an end on January 2, 1781, with a decision by Cornwallis. Morgan had scored again on a marauding band of loyalists near Ninety-six. Cornwallis judged him to be the more dangerous of his two enemies and ordered Tarleton out to drive him north. To Camden he sent Leslie to defend it against Greene. Cornwallis himself then moved stealthily northwestward to impale Morgan as he retreated from Tarleton.

THE COWPENS AND THE COURTHOUSE

Tarleton began the drive with nearly eleven hundred men, and Morgan now had a hundred less. The Americans fell back to a place called Hannah's Cowpens, a corral for cattle near the Broad River. There on January 16 Morgan halted and turned to face the British. On sloping, slightly wooded ground approximately five miles from the river, he arranged his division in three parallel lines. At the rear he hid William Washington's cavalry. In the main middle line he stationed his Maryland and Delaware Continentals, steady veterans all. In front he stretched out the militia under Pickens and asked of them only that they fire two volleys; then they could retire around behind the Continentals and be protected by the cavalry. It was a beautiful setup, and the hardbitten old wagoner waited confidently, spending most of the cold night in reassuring visits among his men.

The British legion appeared next morning after five hours of marching, the dragoons in green jackets, the infantry in scarlet and white.

The War for Independence

"Boys, get up!" Morgan called. "Benny is coming!"

The eager Tarleton rashly ordered his tired men into immediate attack. The southern militia delivered their two volleys with deadly effect, then filed off as if in retreat. Tarleton's troopers charged—straight into the muzzles of the Continentals. The blast stopped them. Before they could recover, Washington's cavalry swept out from behind their hill and fell on the British left. Tarleton threw his reserves into the melee. The Continentals ran forward in a bayonet charge. Morgan now rallied the militia and sent them back under Pickens to break out on the other side of the field and strike again!

Tarleton fled, extricating only 140 horsemen. He squandered 110 killed, 229 wounded, and 600 prisoners: nine-tenths casualties. Cornwallis lost a quarter of his field army. In as brilliant an action as the war produced, Morgan suffered 12 killed and 60 wounded. Equally important, he put his men and prisoners in motion and marched northeastward before slow-footed Cornwallis could get up behind him.

Greene pulled Huger's division back north to consolidate with Morgan and face Cornwallis. In his determination to crush Morgan, the British general called Leslie to join him and destroyed his baggage so that he could march faster. Greene was elated, for now he believed a game of hare and hounds would develop to his advantage. The chase resumed, with Cornwallis under the illusion that he was pursuing a retreating enemy. Tarleton had joined his commander. From Salisbury to Salem to Guilford Courthouse, then northward to the Dan River on the Virginia line, Cornwallis was always on the verge of overtaking Greene but never quite succeeded. Having "pushed" him into Virginia, he dropped back to Hillsboro to rest.

Recovery of the South

Whereupon Greene promptly re-entered North Carolina on February 23 and set about harrying Cornwallis while waiting for reinforcements. Rheumatic and shaking with ague, Morgan had given up and gone home. Changing camp every night, avoiding a general engagement, yet teasing Cornwallis into profitless thrusts, Greene kept the loyalists subdued and raised the spirits of the rebel supporters, practicing "by finesse that which I dared not attempt by force." Early in March he received some new Continentals and fresh militia from Virginia and North Carolina until he had a grand total of 4,400—1,500 of them Continentals (although only 630 were veterans) and the rest militia—more than twice Cornwallis' numbers. Now was the moment to stand and fight, and Greene chose his ground near Guilford Courthouse on March 14.

Taking a leaf from Morgan, he put the North Carolina militia on the edge of a clearing, strengthened at one end by Washington's cavalry and at the other by Lee's. They formed a curved line, and the enemy had to cross an open field to reach them. Greene asked for two volleys from them before they fell back into the woods, where a second line of militia was posted. Behind them and on a low, wooded hill just in front of the courthouse were the Continentals. The three lines were rather far apart, however.

Next day the British approached about noon and formed their lines for attack. As they moved forward the North Carolinians scarcely delivered one volley before running back. The British entered the woods and came under fire from the Virginians as well as the cavalry units. The attack stalled and the fighting was stubborn. Slowly half the Virginia line swung back, like a heavy door being pushed open, and the British on that side surged up to the hill. Boldly they pressed on, the

Continentals waiting for them to come within a hundred feet before they let go a withering blast and then charged down the slope. Nearly every unit was out of position now, and the fighting was widespread, close, and bloody. In desperation Cornwallis ordered his guns to fire grapeshot into the thickest crowd of men, killing his own troops along with the Americans. But the guns forced the latter to withdraw and gave the British a moment to reform. Cornwallis ordered another charge, was thrown back, and both sides took time out. Tarleton had been shot in the right hand and lost three fingers.

Greene found his North Carolinians gone, part of the Virginia militia holding, and the Continentals broken apart. If he had known how badly Cornwallis was chewed up, he could have stood his ground and won. But, never intending to risk destruction of his army that had been so painfully built up, he thought it time to retreat. The disengagement was managed with skill, and the British were too exhausted to pursue. Cornwallis held the field, but he had suffered 25 per cent casualties: 98 killed and 408 wounded. Greene lost 79 killed, 185 wounded, but "missing" were over a thousand North Carolina militia.

For two days Cornwallis rested. Gradually the realization dawned on him that in the word of his day he had been "gulled"—not as badly as that night in January, 1777, at Trenton, but more subtly. Greene had drawn him far from his base of supplies, led him around in circles, and given him a worse beating than Greene had received. Leaving seventy of his critically wounded to the mercies of the enemy, Cornwallis limped back southeast 175 miles to Wilmington, on the coast, where he could get supplies by ship. His withdrawal left the rest of North Carolina open, and Greene with only about fifteen hundred men soon crossed the state southward and headed for Camden, where Lord Rawdon commanded.

Clinton's later acidulous summary of Cornwallis' campaign was not exaggerated:

> After forcing the passage of several great rivers, fighting a bloody battle, and running eight hundred and twenty miles over almost every part of the invaded province at the expense of above three thousand men, he accomplished no other purpose but the having exposed by an unnecessary retreat to Wilmington, the two valuable colonies behind him to be overrun and conquered by that very army which he boasts to have completely routed but a week or two before.

MUTINY OF THE PENNSYLVANIA LINE

Up on the Hudson, Washington put in a restless autumn looking for more French aid and trying to plan a joint campaign. He had to weather one more crisis, however, that was a curious and uniquely American performance. On January 1, 1781, part of Anthony Wayne's Pennsylvania Continentals marched out of their camp near Morristown, New Jersey, and headed for Philadelphia to get immediate action from Congress on their grievances. This was not wholesale desertion but mutiny in a technical sense—a strange kind of military behavior that defied classification.

Their complaints were not of hopes deferred but of justices denied. Although not too badly hutted, they lacked clothing, blankets, and sufficient food, and their pay was in arrears. Wayne wrote on December 16 that in the past forty-six weeks they had received adequate food only a third of the time. Two weeks later he was writing: "The distressed condition of the soldiery for clothing beggars all description. For God's sake send us our dividend of uniforms, overalls, blankets." As the year expired the soldiers had an additional grievance. On January 1 the eleven Pennsylvania regiments were to be reduced to six, incidentally forcing out many officers but keeping all the privates and noncommissioned officers. Those who had enlisted three years before "for three years or during the war" interpeted that oath as meaning no more than three years, contrary to the official view. They passionately wanted to be honorably discharged with pay and clothing so that they might either go home or re-enlist for the new bounties Pennsylvania was offering fresh recruits: twenty-seven dollars in silver and two hundred acres of land after the war. As conditions stood, they could do neither.

January 1 was Wayne's thirty-sixth birthday, and it passed uneventfully in planning the new arrangements. At night the men came out of their huts and talked. They called others out onto the parade and seized the magazine. Refusing to obey their officers or Wayne, they said they were going to Philadelphia. Two officers were wounded and one killed before Wayne gave up his attempt to halt them and meekly followed along with two colonels. A thousand men out of the twenty-four hundred in camp began their march, with cannon, wagons, and fifes and drums waking the countryside.

Arriving at Princeton that night, they made camp while a board of sergeants conducted some negotiations with Wayne. Wayne sent to Philadelphia for civil authorities, and Joseph Reed, now president of the Supreme Executive Council of Pennsylvania, came to Princeton to treat with the sergeants. Meanwhile, the number of mutineers rose by accretion to about seventeen hundred, while others went home from the winter camp, until hardly a hundred loyal soldiers remained there.

Recovery of the South

Both Washington and Clinton heard promptly of the mutiny. The commander-in-chief could not leave his army on the Hudson and recommended that Wayne stay with the troops and negotiate for them with Pennsylvania or Congress. Clinton, without as much hope as some of his officers professed, sent out two emissaries to Princeton with flattering offers if the disaffected troops would join the British. As soon as the emissaries made themselves known, the insulted Pennsylvanians seized them as prisoners.

In negotiation the board of sergeants found itself not in complete agreement, but it demanded and won from Reed discharge of all men who had served three years; acceptance of a soldier's oath over a disputed enlistment date (a score against officers who had deceived their men); arrears of pay to be made up as soon as possible and adjusted to currency depreciation; an immediate issue of shoes, overalls, and shirts; and immunity for all men taking part in the revolt. If this was a victory for the privates, it appears to have been no more than justice. On January 9 they marched to Trenton where the accommodations were to be made. The two British emissaries were delivered up and hanged as spies. Clothing was distributed. Probably a third of the men were entitled to their discharge, but five-sixths swore they deserved it and got it. Many of them asked to re-enlist to get the new bounties, but Pennsylvania lacked the cash in hand; so they went home. Wayne played a difficult role exceedingly well, keeping the respect and affection of the men throughout the ordeal and preventing a bloody resolution of what was actually a sit-down strike. Speaking of "these last twenty tedious days and nights," he wrote to Washington, "I shall only mention that we have not rolled in luxury or slept in beds of down."

The War for Independence

Temporarily the Pennsylvania Line ceased to exist. Its success aroused troops of other states to try similar pressure. Some two hundred New Jersey soldiers from three regiments tried revolt but were suppressed by force on Washington's orders. Two sergeants were executed.

The real culprits were the state governments, which had brought on the trouble by failing to take action. They had repeatedly broken their contracts with the soldiers. The army fared better after the mutiny, partly because the states had become alarmed, partly because the Articles of Confederation went into effect with Maryland's ratification, and partly because of a French gift of money plus a loan. With his unfailing perception and patience, Washington stated the case in his general orders of January 30:

> But while we look to the public for the fulfilment of its engagements, we should do it with proper allowance for the embarrassments of public affairs. We began a Contest for Liberty and Independence ill provided with the means for war, relying on our own Patriotism to supply the deficiency. We expected to encounter many wants and distresses and we should neither shrink from them when they happen nor fly in the face of Law and Government to procure redress. There is no doubt the public will in the event do ample justice to men fighting and suffering in its defence. But it is our duty to bear present Trials with Fortitude, looking forward to the period when our Country will have more in its power to reward our services.

VIRGINIA MAGNET

Washington now had to give his attention to a possibly serious development in the South. If Arnold should be reinforced so that he could overrun Virginia, then Greene would be cut off from communications northward and might be squeezed between Cornwallis and Arnold. Although news of Morgan's victory at the Cowpens relieved Washington, his anxiety returned as Greene fell back before Cornwallis. He urged the French fleet to break out of Newport and descend on Virginia while he sent Lafayette there with land forces. Together they might pinch Arnold off the landscape.

Actually Clinton had not considered a pincer movement against Greene. All he wanted was a naval base established in the Chesapeake from which land forces could operate to cut off supplies to Greene and perhaps move into Pennsylvania in concert with New York troops. He was still counting on Cornwallis to take care of Greene. After Arnold had landed, he had swept up the James River and burned much of Richmond. Steuben removed what stores he could with his few troops. Then Arnold retired to Portsmouth and intrenched. Governor Jefferson, not the military enthusiast that Patrick Henry was, has not escaped blame for the remarkable sluggishness of the state at this time.

Lafayette, at the head of twelve hundred Continentals, reached Maryland in March, 1781. The co-operating French fleet had escaped from Newport and was sailing south. Arbuthnot overtook the squadron off Chesapeake Bay, and in the engagement that ensued the French were worsted and returned to Newport. This was the third disappointment of the French navy.

Immediately Clinton sent Arnold a reinforcement of two thousand men under Major General William Phillips, Burgoyne's old artilleryman (he had been exchanged for General Lincoln) who was also to supersede Arnold as commander. The enlarged task force struck at Petersburg, where much tobacco was burned, and at an anchorage where twenty small ships were captured or burned. Other raids were made until Lafayette moved into Richmond at the end of April. Phillips fell down the river to wait. What he was waiting for turned out to be the culmination of a disastrous decision by Cornwallis.

From his rest camp in Wilmington, Cornwallis with less than fifteen hundred troops did not try to join Lord Rawdon at Camden or to return to Charleston. His mind seemed to be numbed. Finally, on April 23, when he knew Greene was marching against Rawdon, he convinced himself and recommended to Clinton that "a serious attempt upon Virginia would be the most solid plan," since it "would tend to the security of South Carolina and ultimately to the submission of North Carolina." These were almost the same words by which he had justified his move from South to North Carolina. With this specious reasoning Cornwallis turned his back on his subordinates and, without waiting for Clinton's approval of his new move, marched northward across North Carolina into Virginia. On May 20 he joined Arnold (Phillips had just died) and took command of an army that, with a fresh reinforcement, now amounted to seventy-two hundred. Clinton, when he heard, was flabbergasted by this flagrant disobedience of his primary orders to safeguard South Carolina.

HOBKIRK'S HILL

When Greene approached Camden in April he had 1,550 men with him, all Continentals except for 250 North Carolina militia. He felt strong enough to let Marion have the help of Lee's legion, while he retained only Washington's small cavalry unit. His attempt to surprise Camden on the nineteenth failed, and after reconnoitering the vicinity Greene retired to Hobkirk's Hill just north of the town to await Sumter's new corps and the return of Lee, and perhaps Marion with him.

The destination of Lee and Marion was Fort Watson, thirty

miles south of Camden on the Santee River and that much closer to Charleston. It was a stockaded fort built on an old Indian mound and garrisoned by 120 men. Since the Americans had no cannon or intrenching tools, they couldn't lay siege to the place, and, stuck up in the air, it looked impossible to carry by storm. Colonel Hezekiah Maham of South Carolina had an idea for elevating the assault. He took some men into the pine woods, and for five days they cut and notched log timbers. On the night of April 22 they dragged the pieces out to the edge of the fort and proceeded to fit them together into a tower with a platform on top protected by log siding. When dawn broke a company of riflemen started firing *down* on the startled British. While the latter took cover, two other American parties attacked the stockade. Fort Watson surrendered. Then Lee and Marion took off in pursuit of a detachment sent against them by Rawdon.

In Camden Rawdon had only nine hundred men, but he boldly decided to move against Greene's camp. By a circuitous route he came up to Hobkirk's Hill late in the morning of April 25. Greene's advance pickets fell back stubbornly and gave the camp time to form for battle. Greene put his four Continental regiments (Virginia and Maryland) and three cannon into a broad front line, held the militia in reserve, and directed Washington's cavalry to ride around to Rawdon's rear.

Rawdon advanced on a narrow front, three lines deep. Greene began the attack, expecting to fold around the enemy. Rawdon quickly broadened his front by calling up his second line, but his men were falling under the violent rush of the Continentals. Then one of the Maryland companies fell back in disorder after its captain was killed. Colonel John Gunby, instead of rallying it, ordered the whole regiment to withdraw and re-form. This error in judgment opened a hole which the British came whooping through. When the colonel of the other Maryland regiment was hit, his men began to retire. Only the Virginians were holding.

By this time Washington should have struck, but thick undergrowth and fallen trees forced him into a wide arc. He got too far behind Rawdon, swept up some British prisoners, and completed a circle by returning to Greene! He was in time to charge and save the cannon from capture, while Greene ordered a retreat. Rawdon immediately pulled back into fortified Camden, and Greene was able to send back and collect all his wounded. The outcome of the engagement was a humiliating disappointment to Greene because is was so unnecessary. He had lost only 19 killed, 115 wounded, and 136 missing. A court of inquiry blamed Gunby for his "extremely improper and unmilitary" retreat in the midst of battle. But the victory gave little comfort to the British; they had lost 38 killed and 220 wounded and captured, and with Fort Watson gone Rawdon evacuated Camden on May 10 and fell back to within thirty miles of Charleston.

The British still held five other posts in South Carolina, but their days were numbered. Sumter, able, if unco-operative with Greene, captured Orangeburg on May 11. Next day Marion took Fort Motte by the Indian method of setting it afire with burning arrows. Lee seized Fort Granby on the fifteenth, then joined Pickens to lay siege to Augusta, Georgia, with its garrison of more than 600. Meanwhile, Greene had marched west and besieged Ninety-six, which contained 550 loyalists. "Maham's tower" was tried at both places but was successful only at Augusta, which capitulated on June 6.

Lee and Pickens moved up to reinforce Greene. Still they

were unable to crack the defenses of Ninety-six, despite Kosciuszko's parallels and an assault on June 18. A few more days would have starved out the plucky garrison, but Rawdon, having received reinforcements at Charleston, rushed two thousand men west to its relief. Greene withdrew as Rawdon came up on June 21. Lee had already ridden off east to attack Georgetown, but the garrison there hurried down to Charleston on his approach. Two weeks later Rawdon ordered the evacuation of Ninety-six and returned his troops to Charleston. A detachment was left at Orangeburg on the way, but otherwise only Savannah and Charleston were held. The exhausted Rawdon took ship for England and was captured by the French; Lieutenant Colonel Walter Stewart succeeded to the command.

Greene went into summer camp on the High Hills of Santee. Six weeks had passed since he had met the enemy at Hobkirk's Hill, and Cornwallis had marched off to Virginia—to a fateful hamlet he had never heard of called Yorktown.

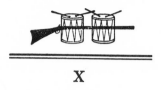

X

Rendezvous at Yorktown

While Greene was reconquering the South in the spring of 1781, in the North, Clinton, with more than his usual confidence, was fashioning two moves to reduce the enemy: defeat and capture of the French squadron at Newport and a pincer movement on Philadelphia by the force under Phillips in Virginia and a detachment from New York City. Both plans, significantly, required recapturing cities previously abandoned by the British. Clinton did not know which action might materialize first, because each depended on the assistance to be given by another commander. For the Rhode Island thrust he must have full naval co-operation, which he knew he would never get until Admiral Arbuthnot was replaced. His alternate plan was upset by word from Cornwallis on May 22 that he was marching up to Virginia to take over command from Phillips, followed by news on June 9 that Phillips was dead and Cornwallis was galloping off in pursuit of Lafayette. The last thing Clinton wanted was to be committed in Virginia. Immobilized and distracted by these circumstances, he began to chafe and complain.

Rendezvous at Yorktown

To Washington, spring brought strains, delays, and discouragement. The states were not sending in their quotas of men, even though Congress had reduced the army to fifty-eight regiments; food was as scarce as ever; when clothing was ready, no teams were available to bring it; the currency had taken a new plunge; and the prospects of the French gaining superiority at sea—on which all Washington's hopes were pinned—seemed as remote as ever. As a result he wrote to the president of Congress that he was unable to plan any campaign.

But early in May, Rochambeau's son arrived in Boston with dispatches from France, and soon Washington was asked to meet with the French general and with the admiral, the Comte de Barras. The place was set at Wethersfield, Connecticut; the date, May 21. There the fresh news was revealed: a large French fleet under the Comte de Grasse, with marines aboard, had sailed from Brest for the West Indies. One ship of the line and six hundred men were going to break off and proceed to Newport. Rochambeau wanted to take the offensive; how could his troops best be used? A joint march to Virginia to drive out Phillips, perhaps?

Washington demurred. He did not yet know of Cornwallis' invasion of the state. He thought the distance so taxing, wagons so difficult to find, and the objective so likely to be thwarted through British mastery of the sea lane that he argued for a joint attack on New York. The same purpose would be answered by forcing Clinton to recall troops from Virginia, removing a threat to Greene. Perhaps Lafayette would be enabled to proceed southward to reinforce him. Washington said he expected to have more than ten thousand troops available in a few weeks.

But what, Rochambeau asked, if Grasse should send part of

his fleet up the coast? This exciting possibility opened up the prospect of winning control of the water, in which event Washington was willing to consider any fresh plan. Before they parted they all agreed that Washington should request the French minister in Philadelphia to urge Grasse to sail north as soon as conditions in the West Indies permitted.

Returning to his headquarters at New Windsor, New York, Washington set about completing plans for a joint attack on New York City. He wrote to Lafayette on May 31 of the decision. Three days later Sir Henry Clinton was reading the captured letter—and foolishly letting his luck be known. Chagrined, Washington felt forced to go ahead with the discovered project anyway. Then he learned of Cornwallis' arrival in Virginia. Greene was now safe, but Lafayette endangered. To give him immediate relief, Wayne's reorganized Pennsylvania Line (amounting to only a thousand men) was sent south, to be followed by a new levy of militia from Pennsylvania, Delaware, and Maryland. Left with only fifty-five hundred Continentals and no militia, Washington began to wonder if, even with Rochambeau's four thousand, New York might prove too much for him. Then on June 13 he heard from Rochambeau that Grasse definitely was coming north—but when or with how many ships remained unknown. Thus Washington found himself in almost the same uneasy predicament as Clinton.

Cornwallis, the man who had peremptorily advised his chief to undertake "solid operations" in Virginia, utilized his new army in chasing Lafayette in much the same manner he had pursued Greene. The nimble Frenchman, with twelve hundred Continentals and as many militia against seventy-two hundred of the enemy, knew what he was doing.

Rendezvous at Yorktown

"I am therefore determined to skirmish, but not to engage too far," he wrote, adding with a wink, "I am not strong enough even to get beaten!"

He had to abandon Richmond as Cornwallis approached and moved northward in a line parallel to the British, holding himself between them and the American supply depots. Cornwallis sent Tarleton clear to Charlottesville in a wild attempt to capture Governor Jefferson and the state assembly. A few legislators were seized, but the cavalry reached Monticello ten minutes too late to find Jefferson. John Graves Simcoe's rangers were also dispatched westward to seize supplies and break up Steuben's troop training, but the baron fled with his new Continentals.

Near Fredericksburg, Wayne joined Lafayette. Six hundred mounted riflemen came in under Colonel Campbell of Kings Mountain fame. Lafayette sent for Steuben and persuaded Morgan to shoulder his rifle again. At this juncture, however, Cornwallis decided he had gone far enough and turned back southward to Richmond. He was finally growing uneasy over what plans Clinton might be formulating and dared not commit his force to battle until he had heard from New York. Lafayette followed the British back to Richmond. When Steuben joined him with 450 Continentals and more militia appeared, Lafayette had a force of 5,200. Cornwallis fell down the peninsula toward the coast. At Williamsburg on June 25 he found letters from Clinton ordering him to take a defensive post and send part of his army back to New York for the projected sweep on Philadelphia.

As the French army prepared to join Washington on the Hudson, he projected a surprise on New York for July 2. His own troops were to descend both banks of the Hudson and meet the incoming French at the point of attack. After the Americans were put in motion, a British foraging party encountered the foremost troops and spread the alarm. The assault failed because Clinton quickly pulled in his outposts behind the Harlem River before the combined forces could strike, but that in itself was a minor success. Washington moved his headquarters down to Dobbs Ferry, thirty miles closer to the city.

Clinton wrote to Germain of the importance of seizing the military stores and supplies at Philadelphia and of his plan to send Major General James Robertson with a thousand men to act in concert with the three thousand under Leslie which Cornwallis would detach. At the same time the exit of the French from Newport, leaving only a small guard, rendered the naval base a "tempting object." On July 4—at last—Arbuthnot was recalled, and the naval command devolved on Vice-Admiral Thomas Graves, who was more agreeable if not more able. In conference with him Clinton pressed for action against Newport. They also discussed Cornwallis and agreed that he should fortify positions at Old Point Comfort and Yorktown; if these works should require use of all his troops, he could keep them until the fortifications were finished. Thus the raid on Philadelphia was quietly postponed in favor of Newport. Then abruptly Graves hoisted sail to intercept a French convoy bringing money to Congress, an unsuccessful cruise from which he did not return until August 16!

Lafayette was following Cornwallis down the peninsula between the York and James rivers. From Williamsburg, Cornwallis, irritated by Clinton's orders, moved south to cross the James River at historic Jamestown. Lafayette hurried up to strike him on the crossing and was informed that only a rear guard remained. Actually, Cornwallis anticipated such a blow and had put only his baggage and a vanguard over the river. The Americans pushed on to Green Spring Farm, early home of Governor Sir William Berkeley, half a mile from the British outposts.

On July 6 Wayne skirmished with some patrols of Tarleton, advancing slowly, unaware that Cornwallis' whole army lay on the other side of a strip of woods. When the rest of the Continentals came up about five o'clock, Cornwallis decided there were enough in view to warrant an attack. His extended front line burst out on Wayne's nine hundred men first and began to encircle them. Perceiving the trap and the odds against him, Wayne feared that a sudden retreat would produce panic. So he ordered an attack! A short, hot fight ensued and then he was able to withdraw in good order to Lafayette's main line. Cornwallis did not pursue but finished his crossing unmolested. Wayne lost twenty-eight killed, ninety-nine wounded, and twelve missing in his narrow escape. The British suffered seventy-seven casualties. Cornwallis headed for Portsmouth, where he could embark some of his troops for New York. His brief, scattering "offensive" in Virginia was finished.

When Washington learned of this move he perceived inviting possibilities if Grasse should enter Chesapeake Bay. But the tempting concentration of British forces on a peninsula could not last, Washington thought; surely Cornwallis would send part of his troops to New York and take another part back to Charleston. Meanwhile, Washington would examine Clinton's defenses by a reconnaissance in force, which he executed on July 22–23 along the Harlem River front. It left him undecided between Virginia and New York City for operations; there were still too many "ifs" in both situations.

The War for Independence

July ran out, and August days turned. Cornwallis now received word that he could hold his troops until his fortified station was completed. He rejected Old Point Comfort in favor of Yorktown and the point across the York River from it, Gloucester. He reported having seventy-five hundred troops and several hundred loyalists consuming his stores; all the troops would be needed to build earthworks in the light soil.

NEW YORK BYPASSED

On August 11 transports entered New York Harbor with twenty-six hundred German reinforcements, raising Clinton's garrison to fifteen thousand. Sir Henry was now more than ready to proceed against Newport—if only Graves would return from sea.

Washington was disheartened by this accretion to the enemy's forces, but suddenly on August 14 electrifying word came from Admiral de Barras at Newport: Grasse was coming—and soon—to the Chesapeake—with thirty ships and three thousand soldiers! Impatient to act, Washington immediately grasped all the potentialities and came to an immediate decision. He rushed word to Lafayette to slip around to the south of Cornwallis so as to prevent his retreat into the Carolinas. He wrote to Barras to load the heavy siege guns and salted provisions and head for the Chesapeake to join Grasse. He conferred with Rochambeau about the march. He put Heath in command of the Hudson and gave him thirty-five hundred men. On August 19, five days after he received the French intelligence, the combined force of twenty-five hundred Continentals under Benjamin Lincoln and the four thousand French was in motion, its secret objective: Yorktown!

Admiral Graves had returned on August 16 from his fruitless attempt to intercept French money to Congress, with two ships in need of repair. Next day Clinton, too, heard that Grasse was on his way north with all his ships and troops—but discounted it as wild rumor. Anyway, even if it should be true, Germain had earlier assured him that in such an event Admiral George Rodney and the British West Indian fleet would be in close pursuit of the Frenchman. Then came intelligence that Washington's troops were moving down the west side of the Hudson. At first Clinton assumed that they must be changing their headquarters to Washington's favorite spot of Morristown, New Jersey. But as spy reports indicated the French were marching too, it became apparent that he must brace himself for the postponed blow at New York. Staten Island was said to be the staging area this time, as the Americans were carrying pontoons.

Then on August 28 Rear Admiral Samuel Hood sailed into New York Harbor with fourteen ships of the line from the West Indies. He brought both bad news and good. Rodney had gone home sick; these were all the ships he had sent in pursuit of Grasse. Hood had looked in at Chesapeake Bay on his way north and had seen nothing of the French fleet. This was frankly puzzling, but he agreed with Clinton that Grasse could not have more than a dozen ships with him. Then came word that Barras had taken his seven ships out of Newport. Not only had the bird flown while Graves dallied, but obviously he was going to a rendezvous somewhere with Grasse. Graves and Hood joined their squadrons and with nineteen sail set off southward on August 31 to find the French.

Still waiting behind his fortifications for the assault that never came, Clinton fumed and slowly learned that he was being ignored by the enemy. On September 2 he wrote to

The War for Independence

Cornwallis a sentence of masterful understatement: "It would seem that Mr. Washington is moving an army to the southward with an appearance of haste." On that very day, indeed, the van of the Franco-American force was pouring through Philadelphia, and Washington had been there for three days. His secrecy and his ruses had worked. His present worry was about Grasse and Barras—and it was groundless. What he did not yet know was that Grasse, having been overtaken and passed unseen by Hood, had arrived safely at the mouth of Chesapeake Bay on August 30 and was sending small boats up to the Head of Elk, less than fifty miles below Philadelphia, to transport the hurrying allies down to the York peninsula. The trap for Cornwallis was already sprung.

Washington received the joyous news on September 5 on his way to Wilmington, Delaware. Making arrangements for embarking as many troops as the boats could take and marching the others, Washington, Rochambeau, Duportail, and their staffs set out by horse via Mount Vernon. On September 14 Washington reached Williamsburg and the welcoming embrace of Lafayette. No, Cornwallis had not escaped. Yes, the troops under the Marquis de Saint-Simon had landed. No, Barras had not arrived. Yes, Grasse had put out to sea to fight the British fleet. No, he had not yet returned.

Graves and Hood had not encountered Barras, but they had no trouble finding Grasse on September 5. The Frenchman sailed out of the bay to meet them at noon with twenty-four ships of the line. Trying to stay between the enemy and the channel of the Chesapeake, he assumed a defensive position. Graves was equally cautious because he was outnumbered. When the wind brought them closer, Grasse opened a heavy fire that lasted until the lines drifted apart. The British lost 90 killed and 246 wounded; the French had 200 casualties. The two fleets maneuvered in sight of each other for the next three days. Graves lost one of his five damaged ships. The fleets moved farther apart in the next two days; then Grasse turned back to the mouth of the Chesapeake on the eleventh. There he captured two British frigates and found that Barras had stolen in the night before. Graves hung around until the thirteenth, his tactics having disgusted Hood, and then headed back to New York. The battle had been small, but it marked all that the navy would do.

Washington soon sailed out into the bay to meet Grasse, taking Knox and Rochambeau with him. The admiral received them on the deck of his 110-gun flagship, "Ville de Paris," the biggest warship afloat. Grasse had already shown he was not a man to do things feebly or by halves, and this was suggested by his stature: he was a giant of a man and demonstrative in Gallic fashion. He already had conceived great admiration for Washington, and when he now saw him he embraced the dignified Virginian, kissed him on both cheeks, and called him "Mon cher petit général!" Washington bore up with his usual poise, but the scene was too much for the amiable Knox. He collapsed in laughter. At the conference, Washington learned he could depend on the French fleet and marines until the end of October. Grasse would also throw two thousand sailors into an assault if necessary, but he would not agree to repeating his performance in Charleston Harbor if Yorktown surrendered before October ended.

The combined armies—fifty-seven hundred Continentals, thirty-one hundred militia, and seven thousand French—moved out of Williamsburg on September 28 and set up camp in sight of Yorktown's seventy houses and buildings. Cornwallis pulled in his advance posts but maintained two stout redoubts on his left, next to the York River. A siege was a formal military business with as precise steps and courtesies as a minuet. Where two armies participated, the formalities were almost overwhelming. Washington won the respect of the French by his knowledgeable precision in conducting operations. He ordered two redoubts built in the sandy soil for cannon which had been hauled down from the Hudson as well as for those which were being unloaded from Barras' ships. A detachment of eight hundred French and some Virginia militia under the Marquis de Choisy was drawing the noose around Gloucester, where Tarleton was stationed.

After some guns were in place Washington ordered the first "parallel" trench to be dug, and the shoveling began on the night of October 6. Next day the trench was occupied and more gun emplacements started. Bombardment of Yorktown commenced on the ninth, the first reply to Cornwallis' fitful firing on his ring of enemies. His earlier show of independent enterprise seemed to have evaporated; all he had left was endurance.

EUTAW SPRINGS AND NEW LONDON

Washington was cheered meanwhile by further news from Greene. After a summer of inactivity in the heat, Greene had put his twenty-four hundred Continentals and militia in motion early in September. Marion, Sumter, and Pickens had joined him. Under Stewart the British to the number of two thousand had moved out of Orangeburg and encamped at Eutaw Springs. On September 8 Greene struck him.

The militia fought well, firing seventeen rounds. Stewart had to commit his reserves. Then Greene threw in his best troops. The stubborn battle developed into a slugging contest that lasted three hours in the middle of the day. Colonel Washington was wounded and half his cavalry were casualties before the British line broke. As the British fled toward Charleston, the Continentals suddenly turned to looting the British stores, ate the food, and drank the rum. Thus complete victory escaped them. Greene called it "by far the most obstinate fight I ever saw," and losses were heavy on both sides. He had 139 killed and 375 wounded. The British counted 84 killed, 351 wounded, and 257 missing, most of them prisoners. Afterward the partisan leaders took away their detachments, and with all his wounded Greene was reduced to a thousand men fit for duty. But the British were now bottled up in Charleston, and Greene settled down before it. His great work was finished after nine months of command in the South.

Up in New York a frustrated Clinton had tried vainly to delay Washington's southward plunge by dispatching Arnold (who had returned from Virginia) to raid New London, Connecticut, on September 6. He sailed up Long Island Sound and landed easily in the town; the defenders had gathered in Fort Griswold. When they were attacked, they so mowed down the British that their subsequent surrender was not accepted. Colonel William Ledyard offered his sword to a British officer and was brutally stabbed with it. At this signal a massacre followed. Eighty-five Americans were killed and sixty wounded, most of them mortally. The town was looted, public buildings and warehouses were set afire, and inevitably much of the town was burned. It was not an important battle, and Clinton accomplished nothing by it, but Arnold blackened his name irretrievably.

Still in the dark about the navy, Clinton finally heard on

The War for Independence

September 17 of the unsuccessful engagement with the French. Not until the nineteenth did Graves limp into port with his damaged ships. Now began a kind of comic-opera series of military conferences within the British command, each one raising more questions and imposing more delays than the last. The navy could not venture out again until repairs were made. In fact, it would not go out until Rear-Admiral Robert Digby had arrived with three more warships. Clinton talked of how to go about reinforcing Cornwallis, as if the French fleet somehow could be penetrated. His leisurely indecision was partly in the tradition of British war-making and partly in the belief that Cornwallis had provisions enough to last until the end of October. And so September expired.

Major General Robertson argued that inaction would certainly doom Cornwallis and probably the whole war; therefore a long gamble on immediate reinforcement or rescue was justified. No one else saw the crisis in quite those intelligent terms, and he did not press his views. Turning to more appealing pursuits, he had "Parties of Girls in the Fort Garden, in the Midst of his own Fears, and the Anxieties of this Hour," according to William Smith, eminent loyalist.

On September 23 an ominous message from Cornwallis was received: "If you cannot relieve me very soon you must be prepared to hear the worst." Graves's ships were still under repair, and a sailing date of October 5 was set. Next day Digby reached port with the three ships to which such exaggerated importance had been attached. He had with him Prince William Henry, George III's younger son who was to become King William IV in fifty years, and two days were given over to entertaining the teen-aged royal visitor.

Digby and Hood were not enthusiastic, to say the least, about embarking a relief expedition with no idea where it might land or how it might escape the French fleet. Then Graves reported that his ships would not be ready until October 8, a date he soon postponed to the twelfth. Hood spoke of a need for him to return to the West Indies; he saw no reason to risk the navy just because Clinton was prepared to risk the army. British headquarters was hardly a place of harmony, and its occasional bursts of energy and anxiety were signs of pulling and hauling rather than accomplishment. With no divination, Clinton foresaw disaster, but stubbornly he persisted in launching something.

"UNREMITTING ARDOR"

Within his fortified lines Cornwallis sat and waited, even more hypnotized than Clinton. If he was not aware of his boneheadedness in abandoning the Carolinas to Greene, he must have realized that he had accomplished nothing during his free weeks in Virginia. Moreover, since he should have known after the sea battle of September 5 that rescue by the British navy was impossible, it ought to have been clear to him that his only chance of saving his army was to break out of Yorktown and race northward. It was pointless to go on strengthening the sandy walls by which he was confining himself. He allegedly did nothing because Clinton had promised him reinforcement or relief. In this listless stupor, the loyalist refugees consumed his provisions, the cavalry horses had to be shot, and smallpox broke out.

On October 11 the allies began digging another trench three hundred yards closer to the Yorktown parapets and in a line pointing toward the two advanced redoubts held by the British. The little forts would have to be taken by assault. The time was set for the night of October 14. The larger redoubt was assigned to the French: four hundred picked troops under Colonel the Marquis de Deux Ponts. Despite an initial barrage, they encountered furious resistance from 120 British and Hessians that cost them 15 killed and 77 wounded in the half-hour before they swept over the stronghold. Four hundred Americans under Lieutenant Colonel Alexander Hamilton attacked the smaller redoubt with bayonets and took it in ten minutes, losing 9 killed and 31 wounded. The second parallel was extended to include both positions before dawn, and the new line was occupied on the fifteenth.

In a forlorn gesture, Cornwallis ordered a sortie before sunrise on October 16. Lieutenant Colonel Robert Abercrombie led 350 grenadiers and light infantry in a dash to the allied trenches, where they inflicted 17 casualties and spiked 6 cannon, suffering 20 casualties themselves, a minor stroke which Cornwallis magnified to 100 enemy casualties and 11 cannon. The guns were working again in a few hours, and the unceasing allied barrage continued as before. By next day, the seventeenth, a hundred cannon were pounding the buildings in Yorktown, and the British were taking shelter underground.

Suddenly a red-coated drummer was seen on the parapet beating for a parley. He couldn't be heard amid the roaring guns, but near him stood an officer waving a white handkerchief. Orders were passed silencing the cannon, and an American ran out to meet the British officer, blindfold him, and lead him into the lines. He carried a message addressed to Washington. It was glorious in its brevity:

Propose a cessation of hostilities . . . to settle terms for the surrender . . . Cornwallis.

Rendezvous at Yorktown

At that same hour in New York the British fleet under Admiral Graves, with Clinton and six thousand soldiers aboard, at last began to drop down the harbor toward the open sea.

Washington granted the armistice, of course, and asked for Cornwallis' proposals. When his lordship sought to have his army sent home on parole not to fight against America or France again (as Burgoyne had bargained), Washington demanded surrender as prisoners of war. Commissioners from both sides met in a Mr. Moore's house on October 18. Meanwhile, the idle soldiers climbed from their earthworks to gaze at each other and listen to their bands play.

When the draft of the articles of capitulation was brought to Washington that night, he went over it carefully, granting some, amending others, and denying only Article 10—the stipulation that "natives" (loyalists) were "not to be punished on account of having joined the British army." Washington objected that this was a civil matter to which he could not assent. He had the papers copied, and early the next morning they were delivered to Cornwallis with orders that they were to be signed by eleven o'clock and the troops marched out to deliver up their arms at two o'clock. The articles came back duly signed by Cornwallis and the senior naval officer commanding the river boats and frigates that remained afloat. Then Washington, Rochambeau, and Barras (who acted for the ill Comte de Grasse) signed. It was done!—except the formalities of surrender.

The French and American troops drew up in two lines running back from the second parallel for half a mile. National and regimental flags were flying, rivaling the yellow, red, and green leaves in the warm October sun. The French officers

179

were immaculate in dress uniforms, their coats all colors of the rainbow. Their troops donned black gaiters below their white breeches. As usual, only part of the Americans had uniforms; most of them wore long hunting shirts. But they were not outdone by the French in dignity and evenness of ranks. They looked unlike any other army in the world. They were lean, hard, immensely self-reliant; durable veterans of defeats and seasons that few professional soldiers would have survived. In truth nothing had daunted them, and now they were reaping a long-delayed reward, brought about by a man who possessed their qualities in a higher degree.

First was heard the music, not marches but melancholy airs, including "The World Turned Upside Down." French or American melodies had been proscribed. At the head of the column rode a British general and his staff. When he came up to the two commanders, he spoke first to Rochambeau, a sly effort to surrender to a French professional rather than a colonial amateur, but with exquisite courtesy the Frenchman pointed across the pathway to Washington. The general turned with an apology and addressed himself to the commander-in-chief. He introduced himself as Brigadier General Charles O'Hara—obviously Irish and about forty years old—representing Cornwallis, who was "indisposed." In the end the aristocrat had taken the cowardly way out. This final insult did not cause a flicker in Washington's poise; he replied that the deputy should speak to General Lincoln, *his* second. Determinedly cheerful, O'Hara moved along to face Lincoln and offered his sword in token of surrender. Lincoln received it and then handed it back, telling him where to lead his men and where they were to stack their arms.

Rendezvous at Yorktown

The British and German troops began passing, many of them in liquor, toward an open field. All of them were sullenly or sadly quiet. Their flags were cased. Some wept, some swore, as they dropped their muskets and moved off to wait internment. Altogether 6,000 surrendered, plus 840 seamen. Across the river at Gloucester, Tarleton surrendered 1,250 more to the allies, and he himself requested protection from American retaliation. In addition the British had 326 wounded, besides 156 who had been killed and 66 missing. The Americans had lost 23 killed and 65 wounded; the French paid more heavily with 60 killed and 193 wounded.

During these same hours, far northward, the British task force stood out to sea on a favorable wind and pointed for the Chesapeake to save Cornwallis.

At the end of the long day, two men began letters to their chiefs. Both opened with directness. One wrote:

SIR,

I have the Honor to inform Congress, that a Reduction of the British Army under the Command of Lord Cornwallis, is most happily effected. The unremitting Ardor which actuated every Officer and Soldier in the combined Army in this Occasion, has principally led to this Important Event.

It was a short letter to mark the climax of Washington's long military exertion, and the credit went to others. The other man wrote:

SIR,

I have the mortification to inform your Excellency that I have been forced to give up the posts of York and Gloucester and surrender the Troops under my command by Capitulation on the 19th inst. as prisoners of War to the combined Forces of America and France.

I never saw this post in a very favourable light. . . .

It was a long letter, and the blame was thrown on others. Cornwallis was especially caustic against Clinton for failing to save him, yet Clinton never accepted responsibility for the box in which his lordship had shut himself.

The subsequent pamphlet battle between the two men may have entertained England, but it ruined Clinton's career. Cornwallis sailed home promptly and was incredibly received as a hero by both ministry and public, a pedestal he did not achieve in America because the loyalists were put in panic by his failure to secure acceptance of Article 10. The earl later redeemed himself by conducting in India a campaign more intelligent than any he had led in America. Clinton never finished excoriating him and left unpublished a history of the war that reviled him anew.

The British rescue fleet reached the Chesapeake on October 26, looked in at Grasse's fleet, and sailed away. Thus came to nothing the weeks of foolish, anxious planning, weeks that blinded Clinton to considering what might have been an effective counterstroke up the Hudson against Heath's small force.

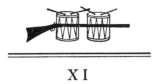

XI

Flames and Embers Extinguished

Washington did not allow himself the indulgence of suggesting or thinking that the war might be over. After all, New York, Charleston, and Savannah remained in enemy hands, and those three places contained a total of twenty-two thousand British and German troops. Moreover, the impending departure of Admiral de Grasse would leave the British in command of the coastal waters once more. Washington warned Congress and the states not to relax their efforts, for the spring might see a fresh offensive.

The French fleet sailed for the West Indies, and Rochambeau remained in Virginia to guard the British prisoners. Washington sent his Continentals back to the Hudson while he himself stopped off to consult with Congress, the result being that he spent the winter in Philadelphia. Lincoln was appointed Secretary at War and took over some of the staff work from Washington, helping him calculate the number of officers needed in 1782 to command the Continental regiments that the states were to fill out.

The War for Independence

Before the army returned northward, St. Clair and Wayne had been detached to join Greene with two thousand Pennsylvania, Maryland, and Delaware Continentals. The reinforcement proceeded slowly, driving four hundred beef cattle, and did not reach Greene until January 4, 1782, at his Round O camp, forty miles from Charleston. Greene immediately sent his friend Wayne into Georgia with troops. A patriot government was promptly re-established. The British kept within the lines of Savannah, but Wayne caught a loyalist detachment trying to arouse the Indians and scattered it. He kept moving about to avoid surprise and to harry any sally parties. Once in June his camp was ambushed by a Creek war party, but Wayne routed it and killed the chief. On July 11 Savannah was evacuated, the thousand British regulars sailing up to Charleston, the loyalists taking refuge in St. Augustine, Florida. Georgia was fully recovered.

Meanwhile, Greene's own troops were living on rice and poor meat. They had received no clothing all winter and no pay for two years. With the onset of warm weather, malaria reappeared in addition to the dysentery induced by their diet. Still, the army confined the British to Charleston and cut off most of the supplies by land, although civilians smuggled provisions into the city to get cash at high prices. Greene was reduced to sending out parties to collect beef and hogs by force. Rum was not to be had at all. The new British commandant, Leslie, sent out occasional foraging parties, and these provoked skirmishes, chiefly with Lee's and Colonel Washington's mounted legions.

The Pennsylvanians grew discontented again, and one of the sergeants who had participated in the earlier mutiny tried to arouse a group of malcontents to seize Greene and other officers and deliver them up to the British. The fantastic scheme being discovered, the sergeant was executed, and a dozen of his conspirators deserted to the enemy.

The war in the West had continued, too. The impetus given Spanish aggression by Governor de Gálvez was maintained. While Gálvez went to Havana to seek reinforcements, Lieutenant-Governor Francisco Cruzat of the Illinois district sent Captain Eugenio Pourée of St. Louis with 66 militiamen and 60 Indians in a dash beyond Lake Michigan to capture the British trading post of Fort St. Joseph (Niles, Mich.) in January, 1781. They looted the place and left immediately, but apparently hoped to establish Spain's claim to the Great Lakes region if the Emperor cared to press it. Gálvez sailed into Pensacola Bay in February, 1782, and prepared to shell the town. Brigadier General John Campbell withdrew to Fort George in an agreement with Gálvez to neutralize the town, and Gálvez' troops landed and laid siege to the fort. The British held out for weeks, until the Spanish guns hit their powder magazine. The explosion killed 105 redcoats. Three hundred of the garrison having escaped to Georgia and 56 having deserted, Campbell surrendered 1,113 as prisoners of war on May 9. The capitulation later cost England both West and East Florida in treaty negotiations with Spain.

George Rogers Clark, now a Virginia brigadier general, still hoped to attack Detroit from Kentucky. In the summer of 1781 he mustered four hundred men at Pittsburgh and descended the Ohio River to Fort Nelson, built at modern Louisville. He was followed by a reinforcement of one hundred and seven Pennsylvanians under Colonel Archibald Lochry. Near modern Aurora, Indiana, they encamped on August 24 and were ambushed by a party of Indians and militia from Detroit.

Thirty-six were killed, and all but two made prisoners. Clark's objective was delayed again, and the Kentuckians urged him to stay on the river as their defensive leader.

The Yorktown defeat made little impression on the British at Detroit, where Colonel Arent de Peyster now commanded. Indeed, the news did not reach that post until April, 1782. The British and their Indian allies still hoped to keep the Americans on the south side of the Ohio River. Border raids were resumed, and American frontiersmen now committed a series of disastrous blunders. A detachment of Pennsylvania militia under Colonel David Williamson in March, 1782, pursued some dusky marauders westward to the Tuscarawas River in Ohio. Losing them, they came upon about one hundred and fifty men, women, and children—Christianized by the Moravians and living a precarious life of neutrality in a village called Gnadenhutten. Williamson showed neither discrimination nor mercy. The Pennsylvanians rounded up more than ninety of the Delawares, packed them into two cabins, then systematically butchered them all.

The frontiersmen still thirsted to carry their warfare to the heart of the savage enemy on the Sandusky River. An expedition of 465 Pennsylvanians and Virginians assembled in May and elected Colonel William Crawford, a retired veteran, to lead them. He marched across eastern Ohio into the Huron, or Wyandot, country. The Indians sent for reinforcements to Detroit and to their neighboring tribes and on June 4 advanced to meet the Americans. About eight hundred Indians and some mounted French militia under Captain Matthew Elliott brought Crawford to a standstill on the Sandusky River and began to surround him. After holding out all the next day, Crawford ordered a retreat in the night. Although only five of his men had been killed in battle, sixty-five were overtaken in pursuit, and the lucky ones were killed promptly. The others, including Crawford, were saved for slow torture and death.

Greatly encouraged, Detroit militia and Indian allies combined to descend on Kentucky again. About five hundred appeared at Bryan's Station (population 90) on August 15, 1782. The plucky defenders held their fort for three days, until the approach of reinforcements seemed to scare off the invaders. The Canadians and Indians withdrew slowly, and 182 aroused Kentuckians under Colonel John Todd pursued them—against the advice of Daniel Boone, who wanted to wait for further reinforcements. Nevertheless, he went along with his neighbors and, at the Blue Licks (southwest of Maysville) on August 19, pitched into an unequal battle. The boastful Kentuckians were routed in a few minutes and driven back in panic across the Licking River. Seventy were killed (including Todd and Boone's son), twelve were wounded, and seven captured.

ECHOES IN LONDON

News of Cornwallis' surrender had reached London on November 25, 1781. Germain carried the dread report to Lord North, who received it "as he would have taken a ball in his breast" but managed to pace up and down crying, "Oh God! It is all over." The less demonstrative King was shocked but naïvely declared he would still prosecute the war. The ministry's majority in Parliament declined as each vote taken revealed growing lack of confidence. Lord Sandwich, who was inclined to take credit in the cabinet for naval victories, blamed the Almighty for the poor showing of the fleet before Yorktown and resigned, to no one's regret.

The Christmas recess gave Lord North's ministry a few

weeks of grace. Clinton, who had been prone to resign his command at the slightest pretext, did not resign after York-town, although he had said he might in an earlier letter to Germain. With Cornwallis removed from the war as a successor to Clinton, the King urged the appointment of Sir Guy Carleton as commander. Since Germain detested Carleton, he recalled Clinton on February 6, 1782, and then resigned. For his dubious services to his sovereign, Germain was created Viscount Sackville. On February 23 Carleton was appointed by Germain's successor to command in America. Then came news of the capture of Minorca by the Spaniards and French. Parliament had no stomach for further warfare. After continued criticism of the ministry's stubborn pursuit of disaster, it voted on March 4 to "consider as enemies to his Majesty and the Country all those who should advise or by any means attempt to further prosecution of offensive war on the Continent of North America." At last Lord North resigned on March 20 and was given a rich sinecure. The distraught King hoped to form a coalition ministry rather than submit to the Whigs he loathed, but failed. He even talked of abdicating, but recovered himself, and Great Britain had him, sane and insane, for thirty-eight long years more.

The Marquis of Rockingham, leader of the opposition, was reluctantly sworn in as prime minister on March 27. He appointed William Petty, Lord Shelburne, colonial secretary and Charles James Fox foreign secretary, both of them long friendly to America. Carleton set off for America in March with orders to fight only if attacked and otherwise to evacuate the troops. He reached New York early in May, and Clinton departed for home to find both a ministry and a public tired of explanations for failure, having heard long defenses from Burgoyne, Howe, and Cornwallis. He was overlooked by the government for a dozen years and then appointed governor of Gibraltar, where he died.

Carleton promptly ordered the evacuation of Savannah and, as soon as it was completed, sent the transports back to Charleston to begin the removal from there. He also wrote to Washington, who had rejoined the troops in the spring, that peace negotiations had started in Paris and that the King proposed to recognize the independence of the thirteen provinces. Suspicious of trickery, Washington forwarded the letter to Congress, which read it as "a matter of information" only, since that body had received no confirming report from Franklin.

Rochambeau began moving his troops northward from Virginia, and a French fleet of thirteen ships of the line under Admiral de Vaudreuil reached the Chesapeake in August. Washington hesitated to suggest any offensive to them. He did proceed with reorganizing the American army into fewer, larger regiments; the indomitable Glover retired, and Gates rejoined the troops as senior major general. When Rochambeau received orders from his king to take his army to the West Indies, he marched them with Washington's blessing to Boston in October to embark on Vaudreuil's fleet.

On September 6 a British fleet had appeared in Charleston Harbor to take off the garrison. Great clamor arose among the loyalists, who feared to remain and yet wanted to carry away their slaves, too. Weeks passed in arrangements.

In the West the war almost flared up again. The defeat at the Blue Licks obliged Clark to retaliate. He gathered over a thousand mounted riflemen at the site of modern Cincinnati and set off for Chillicothe, the rebuilt Shawnee capital. A surprise attack failed, and most of the Shawnee fled before the frontiersmen appeared on November 10. The town was burned, along with five others, and much corn was destroyed. Although only ten warriors were killed, the tribe suffered a severe loss.

On November 14, 1782, a stab of flame shot up from the dying embers. On James Island, South Carolina, Colonel Kosciuszko dispersed a British foraging party and lost five men in the skirmish. This was the last military action of the war.

Not until December 14 were the loaded British ships ready to sail, carrying off about six thousand troops, thirty-eight hundred loyalists, and more than five thousand Negro slaves. Thus the curtain came down on the final act of Cornwallis' stupidity.

THE PEACE TREATY

Wars are sometimes won at the peace table, and the new British ministry hoped to retrieve by adroit diplomacy what it had lost on the battlefield. The best minds of government combined on a plan to separate the United States from its allies, provoke jealousies, draw out negotiations until England's military position improved, and somehow persuade the Americans to accept a loose union with Great Britain. Initial hope was raised by a naval battle between Admiral Rodney and Admiral de Grasse in the West Indies on April 12, 1782, soon after the French had captured two more islands: St. Eustatius and St. Kitts. Departing from traditional tactics of fighting in a line, Rodney broke up the French and won a spectacular victory, even capturing Grasse himself. Then on July 1, Prime Minister Rockingham died suddenly, and Lord Shelburne took his place. His elevation aroused the jealousy of Fox, who resigned.

The United States had selected some able men to represent her as peace commissioners, but John Adams was held up in Holland, John Jay was delayed in Spain, Henry Laurens

Flames and Embers Extinguished

pleaded illness after his imprisonment in London, and Thomas Jefferson was distracted by the fatal sickness of his wife. This left only the aged Franklin to open negotiations. Yet the United States was under no disadvantage, for his talents were equal if not superior to all that Britain could muster against him. While Shelburne pursued his policy, Franklin adopted a countercourse. He almost persuaded Shelburne to throw in Canada as part of the United States before the British position stiffened. What held the two men together was a common belief that both England and the United States would gain most by coming together as friends once more. Hence, all thorns of bitterness were to be pruned away so as to create good will. Independence was recognized in order to draw Franklin away from France and Spain in negotiations. A boundary line up the St. Lawrence, through the upper Great Lakes, and down the Mississippi was drawn, giving the vast trans-Appalachian West to the new country. Franklin could not guarantee to compensate the loyalists for their property losses, but he agreed to have Congress recommend such action to the states. Private debts due British merchants were validated. New England's traditional fishing rights off Nova Scotia and Newfoundland were reaffirmed. It was more than a good treaty for the United States; it was a glorious one.

On November 30, 1782, this preliminary peace treaty was signed, to become operative as soon as England made peace with France and Spain. This task was completed on January 30, 1783, and word was sent to America. When the terms of the American treaty were announced in London, jealous Fox joined the King's friends in denouncing it as conceding too much to the Americans. An unprincipled coalition of Fox and Lord North, recently so hotly opposed to each other, overthrew Lord Shelburne in February, 1783, with the vain promise of procuring better terms. There was neither honesty nor hope in this gesture. The final treaty was rewritten without a change in the terms and was signed on September 3, 1783.

If peace were near, the American officers were growing more resentful about Congress' neglect of them in terms of pay, land grants, and pensions. By March of 1783 this accumulated distress and dissatisfaction produced an anonymous threat to Congress. Washington called a meeting of the officers, made their protest his own concern—tardily, perhaps—in order to direct it, and urged Congress to satisfy their complaints. Congress agreed to continue full pay to officers for five years as a bonus and to privates for four months extra. These certificates for pay were not redeemed for a decade and in the meantime were frequently sold at a heavy discount. Ohio land in hundred-acre tracts was awarded the veterans, its location determined by lottery. Disabled officers were given half-pay for life, and disabled privates were granted a flat five dollars a month. (Not till 1818 were needy veterans of the Revolution allowed a pension, and ten years later all Revolutionary veterans were given a pension equal to their pay and regardless of need. Widows were pensioned later.)

Congress ratified the provisional treaty of peace, and on April 19, 1783—eight years to the day after the skirmish at Lexington and Concord—the cessation of hostilities was formally announced to the army. Washington exerted himself to get at least three months' back pay for the troops, but Congress could not grant even that much. To reduce the daily cost of feeding the men, it directed Washington to grant furloughs and offered the men certificates promising them their overdue pay. The furlough paper automatically would become a discharge when the final treaty was signed. The army marched away by state units, without ceremony or celebration or thanks. As a gratuity the men were allowed to keep their muskets, but many had to sell them on reaching the dispersal center in their state in order to get food or transportation home. Only the three-year men remained in camp on the Hudson. Greene's army broke up the same way, except that the northern units were sent up by ship.

There was one more brief attempt at mutiny. Again it was a Pennsylvania unit on furlough, numbering eighty, that marched on Philadelphia and, joined by other troops in the city, demanded of Congress on June 17 settlement of their debts in twenty minutes! The time limit passed, and the soldiers began drinking. Congress recessed to Princeton, and when General Howe started toward Philadelphia the mutineers moved on to their homes, peaceable but contemptuous of their government. Washington met with Congress late in the summer and was still there in October to welcome Greene. When news came on November 1 of the signing of the final treaty, he rode to West Point.

Carleton had spent the summer of 1783 getting the loyalists out of New York. Many went to Nova Scotia, others to the West Indies, a few to England—all to start over. Parliament granted pensions and compensations generously, but few of the wealthy were restored to their former comforts. Altogether, perhaps eighty thousand loyalists left the colonies during the war and in its closing days. Living up to their convictions was an anguished trial. Those who overcame their preference for monarchy and aristocracy, made peace with their neighbors, and stayed in the United States probably were happier in the end.

The War for Independence

As for the German mercenaries, only 17,300 of the 30,000 employed went home; 7,500 had died, and 5,000 had deserted to remain in a country and a society which they saw were so superior to their own.

The last of the British troops was put aboard transports in New York on November 25. General Knox and a few companies of Continentals swung down Bowery Lane on their heels. The American flag was raised on Fort St. George, and Washington entered the city with Governor Clinton. His mission fulfilled, he wanted most of all to drop his burdens and head for home. On December 4 he met his remaining officers at Fraunces Tavern for a farewell. He toasted them saying:

"With a heart full of love and gratitude, I now take leave of you. I most devoutly wish that your latter days may be as prosperous and happy as your former ones have been glorious and honorable."

Then each man came forward sadly to shake his hand. They followed him out of the tavern, between the ranks of light infantry drawn up as an honor guard, and down to the wharf where, amid a crowd, he boarded a barge for Powles Hook on the Jersey shore. Resuming his journey on horseback, he was accompanied by David Humphreys and Benjamin Walker, his last aides, who were to help him put his papers in order. They trotted over the familiar road across New Jersey, down which he had gloomily retreated in 1776, almost beaten. His route became a series of triumphs as at each town he was greeted and paraded, and he was dined each night.

Approaching Philadelphia on December 8, he was met by President John Dickinson of the State Executive Council, Robert Morris, Generals St. Clair and Hand, and the City Troop of Light Horse. The welcome in the city and the addresses from various organizations overwhelmed Washington; this honor among his fellow citizens was the most satisfying reward he could have had, for it was the one he most desired. He spent a week in Philadelphia, and between receptions and dinners he packed his papers to take to Mount Vernon, bought Christmas gifts, and finished up his accounts for Congress. In 1775 Washington had refused pay for fighting for his country but had accepted his expenses. From time to time he had turned in meticulous accounts of his expenditures; his last one was now received by the treasury comptroller without question.

Washington departed on December 15, was heartily welcomed in Wilmington, danced at Baltimore on the eighteenth, and rode on to Annapolis, where Congress was sitting. President Thomas Mifflin gave him a dinner, and Congress tendered him another one. Again he danced "every set." On December 23 he was to be admitted formally to Congress to resign his commission as commander-in-chief. As one of his last official acts, characteristically, he drafted a letter to Steuben "to express my sense of the obligations the public is under to you, for your faithful and meritorious services."

Precisely at noon Washington entered the Congress chamber with his two aides. The gallery was filled with visitors, but only about twenty members of Congress were in town for this historic session. Charles Thomson, veteran secretary of Congress, escorted him to the front. President Mifflin nodded:

"Sir, the United States in Congress assembled are prepared to receive your communications."

Washington unfolded a paper from his pocket. His hands shook as he began to read:

The War for Independence

"Mr. President: The great events on which my resignation depended having at length taken place; I have now the honor of offering my sincere Congratulations to Congress and of presenting myself before them to surrender into their hands the trust committed to me, and to claim the indulgence of retiring from the service of my country."

There were a few more sentences thanking his comrades in arms, his aides, and Almighty God. He choked and faltered in the sad hush of the room. Then he concluded:

"Having now finished the work assigned me, I retire from the great theatre of action; and bidding an Affectionate farewell to this August body under whose orders I have so long acted, I here offer my commission, and take my leave of all the employments of public life."

Drawing his eight-year-old commission from his pocket, the only man who could have won the Revolution handed it to Mifflin. In 1776 the members of Congress had pledged their lives, fortunes, and honor for independence. Washington had redeemed their pledge. The president responded with a dignified tribute to his leadership and his unfailing respect for Congress. The brief ceremony over, Congress adjourned and each delegate pressed forward to shake Washington's hand. Then, with his aides, Washington mounted at the door and spurred southward. One more night on the road, one more river to cross, and on December 24, 1783, the master of Mount Vernon arrived home, to be embraced by his patient wife and excited grandchildren. He was a farmer once more, the occupation he loved. But now he was also—along with two million of his countrymen—a free citizen of a new nation.

XII

The Summing Up

"If Historiographers," Washington wrote to Greene in 1783, "should be hardy enough to fill the page of History with the advantages that have been gained with unequal numbers (on the part of America) in the course of this contest, and attempt to relate the distressing circumstances under which they have been obtained, it is more than probable that Posterity will bestow on their labors the epithet and marks of fiction; for it will not be believed that such a force as Great Britain has employed for eight years in this Country could be baffled in their plan of Subjugating it by numbers infinitely less, composed of Men sometimes half starved; always in Rags, without pay, and experiencing, at times, every species of distress which human nature is capable of undergoing."

In retrospect, how the foolhardy revolt of 1775 ended in victory and independence still bears the "marks of fiction." The country that lost almost all the battles won the war. It was a contest that Great Britain, in view of her population and strength and preparedness, might have won and should have won. It is foolish to say she didn't try; no one was more intently persistent than George III. It is insufficient to argue that her army and navy were led by more than their fair share of blundering commanders; their ineptness became apparent only in their defeats. Heretofore they had enjoyed high military reputations and were considered amply competent by eighteenth-century European standards. They had simply come up against conditions and opponents that made them look bumbling.

It is easy enough to exercise hindsight and point out some failings of British strategy. Obviously, the army sent to America was not big enough to fight in and occupy the several important areas in the immense battlefield made up of Canada and the thirteen colonies, even though it was a larger army than the Americans could assemble. The British also placed a naïve and fantastic reliance on loyalists, although Clinton finally learned that they were effective allies only as long as a regular army corps remained in their midst. British effort was seriously impaired by lack of unified command, either of scattered armies or of the army and navy. Finally, the officers and men, especially the mercenaries and loyalists, conducted themselves in a manner that rarely encouraged reconciliation but rather aroused a more fierce resistance. The wonder is not that these mistakes were made but that they were not corrected after edifying experience. Persistence in them can only be charged to imperception or obtuseness or inflexibility. Besides these factors that contributed to defeat, campaigning so far from home imposed special difficulties, but this allowance does not explain the American victory either. The United Colonies had their special offsetting weaknesses, too.

WEAKNESSES AND STRENGTHS

Foremost was the distressing fact that the colonial Americans were not united as one voice and one arm in their war effort. A favorite and glib estimate has been that, out of a population of approximately two million whites in 1775 (plus five hundred thousand blacks), one-third opposed the Revolution, one-third was indifferent, and one-third supported it. Perhaps it is based on John Adams' reminiscent opinion that one-third of the population could be classed as loyalists; during the war he once observed that New York and Pennsylvania were almost evenly divided between patriots and loyalists, while New England and Virginia were preponderantly patriot. If one-third of the people (seven hundred thousand) had British sympathies, then two-thirds were either rebels or neutrals. From my own reading, I would guess that seven hundred thousand loyalists is too large a figure, and that more than half the population favored the Revolution. It was a majority rather than a minority movement. Even so, possibly fifty thousand Americans served in the army with British regulars; approximately eighty thousand loyalists went into exile. It should be mentioned here that loyalists were variously motivated and came from all classes of colonial society.

The Secretary at War in 1790 estimated that there had been 396,000 enlistments in the Continental army and state militias during the Revolution. This figure does not mean that that number of individuals served, since many enlisted two, three, and more times. More recent research by the Department of

The War for Independence

Defense indicates that 184,000 to 250,000 men served in the army, navy, and marine corps. Even these estimates seem too high. There could not have been more than 200,000 to 250,000 men of military age, and never more than 30,000 men were in arms at any one time. Probably less than half the manpower, or about 100,000, actually bore arms, many of them under repeated enlistments.

What did the war cost in lives? Available contemporary records yield a conservative estimate of 10,000 to 12,000 fatalities during the Revolution.[1]

The second crippling weakness of the Americans was that the Congress, which could both provoke and declare war, lacked the powers needed to carry on a war. It could not enforce a draft or offer attractive bounties for enlistment. It could not levy taxes to buy equipment, ships, supplies, clothing, and food, or to pay soldiers or prevent inflation. It could not commission generals solely on merit, without considering state

[1] The figure of 4,435 killed has been compiled from records by the Department of Defense and is usually accepted. This sum does not include deaths from illnesses and probably not from wounds. Clarence S. Peterson in his *Known Military Dead during the Revolutionary War, 1775–1783* (Baltimore, 1959) has accomplished the astonishing feat of compiling *by name* a list of approximately 9,500 soldiers and sailors who were killed or died. Clearly, there must be many others whose names are lost. General Gates reported in July, 1776, that the Canadian expedition had cost 5,000 in dead and deserted and that he had 3,000 sick. Even though desertions accounted for the majority, a thousand or two must have perished in this one theater. In the adjutant general's manuscript record at the Clements Library, which runs from March 1, 1778, to June 1, 1783, a total of 4,080 dead may be counted. It is limited to the army under Washington and does not cover the first three years of the war. Dr. James Thacher, a surgeon in the Continental army, estimated total deaths in the war at 70,000! (*A Military Journal* [Boston, 1823], p. 426). Thomas Jefferson, in a letter of June 8, 1778 (*Papers*, II [Princeton, 1950], 197), attempted to tabulate British casualties up to November, 1777, but his figures for particular battles are known to be so exaggerated that his totals are fantastic— 8,844 killed, 11,528 wounded, 9,866 prisoners, totaling 30,238!

The Summing Up

jealousies. Its membership often lacked courage and determination and dispatch in exercising its responsibilities. Congress was obsessed with the problem of proper civil-military relations. In the new republic it feared the army it was compelled to create and controlled it almost to the point of strangling it.

If Americans had been willing to grant authority to a central government, and Congress in turn willing to meet the commander-in-chief's requests, the war undoubtedly would have been shorter and certainly would have been waged more vigorously. Washington remarked after the war that to the defects of the Confederation and the "want of powers in Congress may justly be ascribed the prolongation of the war, and consequently the expenses occasioned by it. More than half the perplexities I have experienced in the course of my Command, and almost the whole of the difficulties and distress of the Army, have their origin here."

A third weakness was the lack of experienced officers. Of course, there was no class of persons indifferent to pay and sensitive to public duty from which to draw them. The British were amused to find American captains and colonels who were artisans and tradesmen. They had no military tradition, no special training, and little experience. Since they must find their own subsistence as well as support their families, inflation or delay in pay forced real hardship on them and drove many of them to resign their commissions unless they had private means of support. To alleviate the situation Washington sought higher pay for officers. "There is nothing," he argued, "that gives a man consequence and renders him fit for Command like a Support that renders him independent of everybody but the State he serves."

It is perhaps not surprising that few first-rate American generals developed under Washington. Greene, Knox, Morgan, and Arnold may be mentioned, and possibly Wayne. The second line of barely competent generals is larger: Howe, Stirling, Sullivan, Lincoln, Glover, McDougall, Hand, and perhaps one or two others. Of the twenty-nine major generals commissioned during the war, five were killed, one turned traitor, two were dismissed, and seven resigned before the end. Half stuck it out. Very few officers ever gave thought to a career in the army because Americans simply were not military-minded and officers were shown no special respect.

In acknowledging these weaknesses, it is not necessary to jump to the opposite extreme and declare that France won the war for us. France's assistance in all kinds of supplies, in cash and loans, and finally in ships and troops was of immense and even decisive help, but it was all predicated and carried out on the basis of sustaining and aiding a fighting American army. Whether Americans could have won the war without French aid is one of those imponderables of history. Undoubtedly the war would have been an endurance contest, and unless Great Britain had put forth greater effort than she ever had, under generals more brilliant than she had found to send to America, she might well have given up the endless fire-fighting that never prevented new flames from starting. Equally possible, the Americans might have become exhausted, and especially through inflation the mighty struggle might have ground to a halt. Still, the crisis of failure or armistice might have rallied a new united effort under a Congress of broader powers.

Yet we won! Of course, British weaknesses helped, but that is only what may be said of any war: the enemy must have been the weaker, or he would have won. Of course, French help was a considerable factor in our success and indispensable

The Summing Up

at Yorktown. But what sustained the American effort, nurtured and strengthened it, and ultimately brought it to victory? We cannot give the credit to a preponderance or even an adequacy of supplies or to better equipment; even the superior Pennsylvania rifle was scarce and not a universal American weapon. No, the enemy was as well armed and much better supplied and clothed. The answer is not to be found in matériel at all. Therefore it must be looked for in intangibles—ideals, faith, self-sacrifice, determination.

First of all, the dedication and perseverance of a few leaders bolstered enough others to maintain an unequal struggle for eight years. These resolute individuals were found in Congress, in state assemblies, in shops, on farms, and in the army. They exerted themselves unselfishly for the cause; they rallied the weaker to their support; they neutralized the objectors. They were the doers, who gave direction and force to the contest. To them independence and freedom had vivid and personal meaning for human life, whether or not all of them could convey their philosophy to others. There were enough of them— and many are not known by name—to keep the country actively at war. They had pledged their lives to win, and they meant it.

Second, a hard core in the army were better fighters than the enemy because of higher morale. The British fought for their king as a reflex conditioned to tradition, not out of personal enthusiasm or respect for his wisdom. Under a strict discipline by an officer caste they could not enter, though generally content with their social status, they fought in obedience to orders and often only to protect themselves from the enemy. They fought well because they had been trained professionally. Although they were more enlightened politically than the

The War for Independence

Germans, neither group comprehended or inquired as to what the Americans were fighting for. The Declaration of Independence made no impression on them. In contrast, several of the aristocratic French officers absorbed some of the American fire and became leaders in the French Revolution.

The American in arms was a citizen-soldier. He had volunteered because he had an idea of how his political life should be ordered. He introduced a new concept into war: patriotism. His loyalty was to his state or to the united states, in contrast to the Briton and German whose loyalty was to a ruler. The American's own honor was at stake. He was fighting to determine the destiny of his country and therefore of his children. Once he received some military training, he usually could defeat the professional soldier and the mercenary because he had higher motivation, more initiative, and greater hope. These embattled farmers and artisans fought as men possessed—possessed of a fervent and ennobling desire to be free men. Already an "American way of life" was as apparent to Americans as it was to a few perceptive foreign observers. This way, moreover, was superior to that of Europe in the opportunities it offered the common man and in its loftier moral standards, politically and personally. It was something to preserve and extend; defeat meant turning back the clock to Europe's time.

Because they were not professional in their tradition, the American soldiers did not react according to the rules of European warfare. Although the British commanders in America recognized this "stubbornness," the ministers in London never ceased to be astonished and exasperated by it. Thus, Germain could not understand why, immediately after a victory, the commander-in-chief called for more reinforcements, just as if he had suffered defeat. The plain fact was that a military victory meant little unless British arms could then occupy and control the area bought by the battle. Consequently, the greater the success in the field, the more troops that were needed to hold what was won. In London this sequence made no sense. But in America civilians of an invaded region would risk their lives to fire on enemy troops—a behavior that was incomprehensible to Europeans. Why wouldn't the defeated Americans stay beaten? The answer was that England was fighting not just another army, but a people.

Finally, America had George Washington as commander of its military forces. His concept of the importance of maintaining an army in revolt and his protection of that army against severe risks have been mentioned earlier. He was a great leader rather than a brilliant general, but he waged a kind of war that brought the downfall of his opponents. In brief, he was better at his kind of warfare than the British generals were at theirs—this in spite of never having all at one time the essentials he needed to deliver a decisive blow. On top of his responsibilities his minor duties were crushing, his correspondence staggering—all of it staff work for a staff he never had. He accomplished it all by driving himself relentlessly; he took no furloughs and suffered only three brief illnesses.

If he were not a warm, jovial extrovert, he yet bound men to him by his deep sense of justice, his magnanimity, and his undeniable aura of leadership. As with most men long dead and pictured in formal portraits at a late age, it is not easy to recall that George Washington was a man of rare personal charm. Although not possessed of a great intellect for abstract thinking, he still could analyze information and arrive at judgments that were penetrating and sound.

Nor could the British understand him. His ethics were incomprehensible in the corrupt world of official London. His amazing perseverance indicated that whatever he must want out of rebellion, the British had it not in their power to give him. That a man could be defeated again and again without being conquered frankly puzzled them.

Whence came his strength is not easy to declare. Certainly it was not religious fervor, although he held an abiding faith that Providence was concerned for America's struggle. Nor was he ahead of his time in hailing the wisdom of the common man to govern himself always with judiciousness and good will. Washington believed in a republic, in government for the people by responsible representatives, not in democratic equality. What he did have in abundance was a patriotism running pure and deep that dedicated him to his duties, a courage and patience that upheld him against despair, and a sense of honor: an image of how he must act to gain his own approval and that of upright men. Small wonder that he enjoyed less than four years at Mount Vernon before again being called to serve his countrymen.

His deference to Congress kept civil authority supreme in the land, and he contemptuously rejected the suggestion that he might establish a military dictatorship. It was his character that prevented the Revolution either from failing or from ending in tyranny and excess. No revolution since that time has been so successful in achieving its original aims.

LESSONS AND MEANINGS

The American Revolution exposed certain inadequacies in Europe's military thinking. The revelation that competent officers could rise from a society without an aristocracy was disconcerting to say the least, and it also exposed the evil of

The Summing Up

the purchase system in making promotions. Equally alarming was the discovery that a republican army made special targets of opposing officers. The massed ranks of European armies were trained to shoot only at other massed ranks. By a kind of silent agreement officers had spared officers on either side.

Wars between professional troops became a phenomenon of the past. Napoleon remembered the American example and formed massive armies by drafting his docile citizens. War was on its way to becoming a total commitment, and its seasonality diminished as winter campaigns grew both desirable and possible.

The rifle was perceived to be the great infantry weapon of the future. Its eventual adoption meant the training of marksmen who could be expected to hit what they aimed at, and the obsolescence of firing volleys by platoons. Concomitantly, light infantry were the foot soldiers of the future, although Britain was slow in recognizing them. These developments required changes in tactics that outmoded the practices of Frederick the Great and deposed him as the military arbiter of Europe.

Admiral Rodney's flexible tactics in defeating the French appealed to one of his captains, Horatio Nelson, who was to develop new methods of naval attack on Napoleon's fleets. Otherwise, British naval service remained as unpopular as ever, and crews had to be completed by press gangs. The United States had learned the ineffectiveness of state navies and realized that privateers drained off able seamen. It evaded the problem by dissolving the Continental navy completely. The need, even necessity, of closer co-operation between army and navy was obvious in both countries, but little was accomplished toward unified command.

The War for Independence

There were little lessons, too. The Americans' lack of colorful uniforms made them less conspicuous in the field, but Europeans hated to sacrifice their bright fabrics. Similarly, American arms rarely reflected sunlight because the men did not spend time polishing them, yet burnishing weapons remained a time-honored boondoggle of European privates.

New England's belief in equality, which was so upsetting to the establishment of order and discipline, nevertheless had the effect of causing the common soldier to be treated with more consideration than he received in any other army. Steuben supported this attitude in his manual for officers. For the first time, privates were permitted to wear "service stripes" showing years of service and good conduct. Yet militarism was not allowed to acquire glamor in America. Standing armies were abominated as economically non-productive and politically dangerous. State militias were relied on, and the few federal troops necessary to guard federal property and the frontier were kept under civilian control.

This narrative must end with the peace treaty that launched a new nation, a people that had turned away from Europe in the very act of emigrating here—in fact, had turned a corner and taken a new road. They had achieved independence, which to many minds meant freedom from restraints imposed upon them. But social order had another face, too, and four years more of disintegrating "freedom" from responsibility would make them alive to their interdependence and to the lesson that they must bear restraints or live in anarchy. Nurtured as they were in religion, Americans were possessed of uncommon spiritual insight; they found that bonds of mutual respect were no harder to shoulder than obligations of love. The movement toward a written constitution of national government, following the examples set by the states, was a culmination of the Revolution—but that is another story.

Some of the war veterans sought new homes across the mountains, where their muskets served again, against the Indians in the 1790's and even in the War of 1812. Their graves are found all the way to the Mississippi. The noise of battle has faded, and the smoke long since blown away. A few cannon are found only in museums; Valley Forge, Yorktown field, and the Morristown camp are national parks. Yet in the haunting echoes of Paul Revere's alarm in the night, of Henry Knox's booming voice in the blizzard on the Delaware's dark shore, of the cheers of Morgan's riflemen at Bemis Heights, of the crashing timbers aboard the "Bonhomme Richard," of the shouts of frontiersmen atop Kings Mountain, of the thundering hoofs of Lee's legion across South Carolina, of the quiet authority of Washington's commands at Yorktown—in all these the wonder of the achievement is evoked. And the great lesson, the final discovery of the Revolutionary generation in its search for political order, is revealed to us: that although the first payment for freedom is courage, the instalments due to keep it are unity and vigilance.

Bibliographical Notes

The military side of the American Revolution has not been neglected by writers. Starting with narratives and defenses written before the war ended, the output of war literature has been steady and profuse. Battles and campaigns have been lovingly recounted by academic, local, and self-appointed historians. A good deal of reminiscence, folklore, and special pleading inevitably has swept into the tide of narration. New England authors rather dominated the field at first, with the result that the first year of the war and the northern campaigns for a long time overshadowed the rest of the war. Unfortunately, no one in the nineteenth century of the stature of Francis Parkman or William H. Prescott took the American Revolution for his life-work. George Bancroft, John Fiske, and editor Justin Winsor produced readable and generally reliable accounts incident to studying larger areas and longer periods.

Meanwhile, letters and biographies of early Continental Congressmen and of generals began to appear in single volumes and in sets. B. F. Stevens provided twenty-six volumes of *Facsimiles of Manuscripts in European Archives Relating to America, 1773–1783* (London, 1889–95). From this growing fund of relevant material at the turn of the century, Sir George Otto Trevelyan wrote four volumes on *The American Revolution* (New York, 1899–1907) that are still a classic work and easily the best study by a British historian.

Manuscript collections continued to pass into institutional care

210

and become generally accessible. The Historical Society of Pennsylvania was given the Anthony Wayne papers in 1890. The Massachusetts Historical Society acquired the Henry Knox papers in 1910, but its John Adams papers, besides those published, were held in trust and did not become fully available until filmed in 1954. John Sullivan's papers were published in three volumes from 1930 to 1939. Important documentary publications appeared in this century. The *Journals of the Continental Congress, 1774–1789* were printed in thirty-four volumes from 1904 to 1937. *Letters of Members of the Continental Congress* were edited in eight volumes from 1921 to 1936. The *Correspondence of King George the Third* (six vols. to 1784) appeared in 1927–28. The complete *Writings of George Washington* were finally issued in thirty-nine volumes, edited by John C. Fitzpatrick, from 1933 to 1944.

Curiously, some of the most pertinent source material did not come to light until the 1920's and early 1930's, when William L. Clements brought to the library he had established at the University of Michigan six great manuscript collections: the papers of Lord George Germain, colonial secretary, 1775–82; of Lord Shelburne, prime minister during the peace negotiations; of General Thomas Gage, British commander-in-chief in North America, 1763–75; of Sir Henry Clinton, commander here, 1778–82; of General Nathanael Greene, American commander in the southern theater; and the letters and diaries of the Hessian officers sent to Baron von Jungkenn, war minister of Hesse-Cassel. At the same time John D. Rockefeller, Jr., acquired for Colonial Williamsburg, Inc., the papers of Sir Guy Carleton, commander in Canada and last commander-in-chief in America, 1782–83. (The collection was presented to Queen Elizabeth in 1957 and returned to England.) Sources for the British side of the war in correspondence and maps were at last available to American historians, and, altogether, great riches were laid before Revolutionary scholars.

The first historian to make use of some of the new manuscripts was Professor Claude H. Van Tyne, whose *War of Independence* (Boston, 1929) received the Pulitzer Prize, the next year, after the author's untimely death. Unfortunately, this volume ended with the beginning of 1778. It is actually in the last decade that the best general histories of the Revolution have appeared: John C. Miller's

The War for Independence

Triumph of Freedom, 1775–1783 (Boston, 1948); Willard M. Wallace's *Appeal to Arms* (New York, 1951); Lynn Montross' *Rag, Tag and Bobtail* (New York, 1952); Volumes III–V of Douglas Southall Freeman's monumental biography of *George Washington* (New York, 1951, 1952); John Richard Alden's *The American Revolution* (New York, 1954); and *Rebels and Redcoats* (Cleveland, 1957) by George F. Scheer and Hugh F. Rankin. All these made use of the newer manuscript resources. The authors have influenced me, I am sure, but in my fortunate location at the William L. Clements Library I have also gone back to the sources they used.

The following bibliographical notes are highly selective. I have not repeated in them all the manuscript collections in the William L. Clements Library, although they have been helpful in almost every chapter. The books cited are for the inquiring reader and indicate the ones I found most useful and consider most authoritative. Many other titles on the regions and periods concerned might be listed.

CHAPTER I

The undisputed authority on the Lexington and Concord skirmishes, Bunker Hill, and the siege of Boston is Allen French, whose long and devoted research is summed up in *The Day of Lexington and Concord* (Boston, 1925) and *The First Year of the American Revolution* (Boston, 1934). Of course, he lists the numerous references on this period and discusses conflicting evidence. Additional light may be found in John R. Alden, *General Gage in America* (Baton Rouge, La., 1948). Edward E. Curtis, *The Organization of the British Army in the American Revolution* (London, 1926) is standard in its field, but chapter iii of Walter Dorn's *Competition for Empire, 1740–1763* (New York, 1940) comments on the quality of recruits.

CHAPTER II

The best account of the Montgomery-Arnold invasion of Canada is still J. H. Smith's *Our Struggle for the Fourteenth Colony* (New York, 1907) in two volumes. Arnold's expedition is detailed in Smith's *Arnold's March from Cambridge to Quebec* (New York, 1903) and in Kenneth Roberts' *March to Quebec* (New York, 1938). For a more general treatment, see George M. Wrong, *Canada and*

Bibliographical Notes

the American Revolution (New York, 1935). Allen French's second title cited in notes to chapter i covers part of this chapter. *A Narrative of Sir Henry Clinton's Co-operation with Sir Peter Parker* (n.p., n.d.) along with William Moultrie's *Memoirs of the American Revolution* (New York, 1802), Volume I, are printed sources for the attack on Charleston.

CHAPTER III

A number of contemporary pamphlets critical of Howe's campaign were published in London; Howe's *Narrative* (London, 1780) is his defense. Troyer S. Anderson's *Command of the Howe Brothers during the American Revolution* (New York, 1936) is an able study by a trained historian. Leonard H. Lundin, *Cockpit of the Revolution* (Princeton, 1940) is a careful account of New Jersey as a battlefield. Henry P. Johnston, *Campaign of 1776 around New York and Brooklyn* (Brooklyn, 1878); William S. Stryker, *Battles of Trenton and Princeton* (Boston, 1898); Alfred H. Bill, *Campaign of Princeton, 1776–1777* (Princeton, 1940); and Bruce Bliven, Jr., *Battle for Manhattan* (New York, 1956) are examples of good local history. Professor William B. Willcox discusses strategy in "Why Did the British Lose the American Revolution?" *Michigan Alumnus Quaterly Review*, LXII (August, 1956), 317-34. The best account of Arnold at Valcour Island is to be found in Kenneth Roberts' historical novel, *Rabble in Arms* (New York, 1933).

CHAPTER IV

Howe's *Narrative*, cited in notes to chapter iii, and Burgoyne's *A State of the Expedition from Canada* (London, 1780), along with the Baroness von Riedesel's *Letters and Memoirs Relating to the American War of Independence* (New York, 1827), are basic to this campaign. Hoffman Nickerson made good use of them in *The Turning Point of the Revolution* (Boston, 1928). Troyer S. Anderson's book, cited in notes to chapter iii, is again relevant and reliable. Edward J. Lowell, *The Hessians and the Other German Auxiliaries of Great Britain in the Revolutionary War* (New York, 1884) is still good but should now be supplemented by the Baurmeister letters in Bernhard A. Uhlendorf's *Revolution in America* (New Brunswick, N.J., 1957). Samuel W. Patterson's *Horatio Gates* (New York, 1941) casts the most favorable light on the general.

213

The War for Independence

CHAPTER V

Perspective on the "winter of discontent" is found in Alfred H. Bill, *Valley Forge: The Making of an Army* (New York, 1952). The suffering of the troops is recounted in chapter xiv of Lynn Montross' *Rag, Tag and Bobtail* (New York, 1952) and in chapters xxiii and xxiv of *Rebels and Redcoats* (Cleveland, 1957) by George F. Scheer and Hugh F. Rankin. The maneuvering for the French alliance is part of Carl Van Doren's *Benjamin Franklin* (New York, 1938), Verner W. Crane's *Benjamin Franklin and a Rising People* (Boston, 1954), and Samuel Flagg Bemis' *Diplomacy of the American Revolution* (New York, 1935). The fairest résumé of the Conway-Gates affair is found in chapter xxiii, Volume IV, of D. S. Freeman's *George Washington* (New York, 1951). Sir Henry Clinton tells his story in *The American Rebellion* (New Haven, 1954), his narrative as edited by William B. Willcox. Lee's incompetence shows up in the *Proceedings of a General Court Martial of Major General Lee* (Philadelphia, 1778). The battle is also reviewed in William S. Stryker and William S. Myers, *The Battle of Monmouth* (Princeton, 1927), and in John R. Alden's *General Charles Lee, Traitor or Patriot?* (Baton Rouge, La., 1951). The Carlisle Commission is examined in Alan S. Brown, "The British Peace Offer of 1778," *Papers of the Michigan Academy of Science, Arts and Letters,* XL (1955), 249–60. Sources for the Rhode Island fiasco appear in *The Letters and Papers of Major General John Sullivan* (Concord, N.H., 1930–39), in the *Diary of Frederick Mackenzie* (Cambridge, Mass., 1930), and in chapter iv, Volume II, of G. W. Greene, *Life of Nathanael Greene* (New York, 1871).

CHAPTER VI

The second British invasion of the South and the second failure of Estaing are discussed in Alexander A. Lawrence's *Storm over Savannah* (Athens, Ga., 1951) and Christopher Ward's *War of the Revolution* (New York, 1952), Volume II, chapter lix. The George Rogers Clark papers were published in the *Illinois Historical Collections* (Urbana, 1912, 1926), Volumes VIII and XIX, edited by James A. James. Hamilton's journal was edited by John D. Barnhart in *Henry Hamilton and George Rogers Clark in the American Revolution* (Crawfordsville, Ind., 1951). The whole episode is well told in Milo M. Quaife's *The Capture of Old Vincennes* (Indianapolis, Ind., 1927). The New York frontier raids are described in Howard Swiggett's *War Out of Niagara* (New York, 1933) and *Journals of the Military Expedition of Major General John Sullivan* (Auburn, N.Y., 1887). British and Spanish action on the Mississippi and in Florida is explained in Volume II of Alcée Fortier's *A History of Louisiana* (New York, 1904), in Charles L. Mowat's *East Florida as a British Province, 1763–1784* (Berkeley, Calif., 1943), and in Cecil Johnson's *British West Florida, 1763–1783* (New Haven, Conn., 1943).

CHAPTER VII

A new naval history of the Revolution remains to be written. Meanwhile, recourse may be had to Gardner W. Allen's *A Naval History of the American Revolution* (2 vols.; Boston, 1913). Alfred T. Mahan's *The Major Operations of the Navies in the American War of Independence* (Boston, 1913) gives little space to the U.S. Navy. Edgar S. Maclay's *History of American Privateers* (New York, 1899) shows good use of records. Admirers of John Paul Jones should not miss Gerald W. Johnson's lively *The First Captain* (New York, 1947). Pierre Landais's aberration is confirmed in his *Memorial* (New York, 1784) and *Second Part of the Memorial* (New York, 1785). The Massachusetts expedition is narrated in John Calef, *The Siege of Penobscot by the Rebels* (London, 1781). Alexander A. Lawrence's book, cited in notes to chapter vi, tells of the siege of Savannah. *Memoirs of the Life of Captain Nathaniel Fanning* (New York, 1808) includes his services in the Revolution. Samuel Eliot Morison has done a careful job on *John Paul Jones, a Sailor's Biography* (Boston, 1959).

CHAPTER VIII

Wayne's exploit was studied by Henry P. Johnston for his *The Storming of Stony Point* (Washington, D.C., 1900). An excellent account of inflation is found in chapter xxii of John T. Miller's *Triumph of Freedom* (Boston, 1948). A fresh study of the Charleston siege was made by William T. Bulger, Jr., "The British Expedition to Charleston, 1779–1780" (Ph.D. dissertation, University of Michigan, 1957). For the Hessian point of view, see Bernhard A. Uhlendorf, *The Siege of Charleston* (Ann Arbor, Mich., 1938). In briefer

The War for Independence

form George W. Kyte discussed the "British Invasion of South Carolina" in *The Historian*, XIV (Spring, 1952), 149–72. Sir Henry Clinton's version of what he did is detailed in *The Amercan Rebellion*, mentioned earlier (notes to chap. v). Banastre Tarleton made sure his exploits would not be forgotten in *History of the Campaigns of 1780–1781* (London, 1787). Arnold's treason forms a large part of Carl Van Doren's *Secret History of the American Revolution* (New York, 1941) and is the subject of James T. Flexner's *The Traitor and the Spy* (New York, 1953).

CHAPTER IX

The disaster at Camden is related in Otho Williams' narrative in William Johnson's *Sketches of Nathanael Greene* (Charleston, 1822), Appendix to Volume I; in Edward McCrady's *History of South Carolina in the Revolution, 1775–1780* (New York, 1901); and in Henry Lee's *Memoirs of the War in the Southern Department* (Philadelphia, 1812). Tarleton's *History*, cited in notes to chapter viii, is useful here, as well as J. G. Simcoe's *Journal* (Exeter, England, 1787). Lyman C. Draper devoted a book to *King's Mountain and Its Heroes* (Cincinnati, 1881). The Virginia campaign is traced in Louis Gottschalk's *Lafayette and the Close of the American Revolution* (Chicago, 1942). The best account of rebellion within the American army is Carl Van Doren's *Mutiny in January* (New York, 1943). Greene's exploits, besides being revealed in his papers, are described in Volume III of G. W. Greene's *Greene* and in several chapters of Volume II of Christopher Ward's *War of the Revolution*. Don Higginbotham's *Daniel Morgan, Revolutionary Rifleman* (Chapel Hill, 1961) is the first biography in more than a century.

CHAPTER X

The old basic account of the Yorktown victory has been Henry P. Johnston's *The Yorktown Campaign* (New York, 1881). It has been largely superseded by Louis Gottschalk's work cited in notes to chapter ix; William B. Willcox, "The British Road to Yorktown: A Study in Divided Command," *American Historical Review*, LII (October, 1946), 1–35; Freeman's *Washington*, Volume V; and Sir Henry Clinton's account in *The American Rebellion* (cited in notes to chap. v). See also Randolph G. Adams, "A View of Cornwallis' Surrender at Yorktown," *American Historical Review*, XXXVII

Bibliographical Notes

(October, 1931), 25–49. Tarleton's *History*, already mentioned (notes to chap. viii), is useful. French activities are recounted in Rochambeau, *Relation, ou Journal des opérations du corps français* (Philadelphia, 1781); Chastellux, *Voyages* (Paris, 1786); and Deux Ponts, *My Campaigns in America* (Boston, 1868). Several manuscript journals by French officers with Grasse are in the Clements Library. The pamphlets issued by Clinton and Cornwallis were gathered by B. F. Stevens and reprinted in *The Campaign in Virginia, 1781* (London, 1888).

CHAPTER XI

Sources for the closing skirmishes in the South are G. W. Greene's *Greene*, Volume III; Edward McCrady's *History of South Carolina in the Revolution, 1780–1783* (New York, 1902); Henry Lee's *Memoirs;* and Miecislaus Haiman, *Kosciuszko in the American Revolution* (New York, 1943). The treaty negotiations are summarized in V. W. Crane's *Franklin*, already mentioned (notes to chap. v). Washington's last months of command are followed in Freeman's *Washington*, Volume V. The expiring war in the West is related in C. W. Butterfield's *An Historical Account of the Expedition against Sandusky* (Cincinnati, 1873); Louis Houck's *The Spanish Regime in Missouri* (Chicago, 1909), Volume I; and John Bakeless' *Background to Glory: The Life of George Rogers Clark* (New York, 1957). Treatment of veterans is discussed in Dixon Wecter's *When Johnny Comes Marching Home* (Boston, 1944), Part 1.

CHAPTER XII

Freeman interprets Washington's value to American victory in chapter xxix, Volume V, of his *Washington*. Willard Wallace discusses the effects of the Revolution in chapter xxiii of his *Appeal to Arms* (New York, 1951). Alfred Vagts's *A History of Militarism* (New York, 1937) touches on the influence of the Revolution on military thought and practice in chapter iii.

Important Dates

218

Important Dates

Burgoyne checked at Freeman's Farm, September 19

Surprise attack on Americans at Paoli, September 20

Howe occupies Philadelphia, September 26

American disappointment at Battle of Germantown, October 4

Burgoyne turned back at Bemis Heights, or second battle of Freeman's Farm, October 7

Burgoyne surrenders at Saratoga, October 17

Amazing defense of Fort Mercer, October 22

Fort Mifflin captured by British, November 15

Washington goes into winter quarters at Valley Forge, December 18

1778   Franco-American alliance signed in Paris, February 6

Drawn Battle of Monmouth, June 28

G. R. Clark seizes Kaskaskia, July 4

Wyoming Valley massacre, July 4

Disappointing Battle of Rhode Island, August 29

Cherry Valley massacre, November 11

British occupy Savannah, December 29

1779   G. R. Clark captures Vincennes, February 23

Spain enters the war, May 8

Battle of Stono Ferry, June 19

Wayne takes Stony Point, July 15

Massachusetts expedition against Penobscot Bay fails, August 13

Sullivan defeats New York Indians at Newtown, August 29

Engagement between "Bonhomme Richard" and "Serapis," September 23

Franco-American attack on Savannah repulsed, October 9

British task force sails for Charleston, December 26

1780   Spaniards take Mobile, March 14

Charleston falls to British siege, May 12

Bird's raid on Kentucky, June 20–28

Rochambeau's French troops arrive at Newport, July 11

Gates defeated at Camden, August 16

Decisive British defeat at Kings Mountain, October 7

1781   Mutiny of the Pennsylvania line, January 1

Morgan's victory at the Cowpens, January 17

The War for Independence

Greene and Cornwallis battle at Guilford Courthouse, March 15

Greene forced off Hobkirk's Hill, April 25

Augusta recaptured, June 6

Unsuccessful siege of Ninety-six, May 22–June 19

Wayne takes on Cornwallis at Green Spring Farm, July 6

French fleet drives British fleet away from Chesapeake Bay, September 5

Arnold's raid on New London, September 6

Greene drives British from Eutaw Springs, September 8

Cornwallis surrenders at Yorktown, October 19

1782 Carleton appointed commander-in-chief to replace Clinton, February 23

Lord North resigns as prime minister, March 20

Spaniards capture Pensacola, May 9

Crawford defeated at Sandusky, June 5

Savannah evacuated by British, July 11

Kentuckians overwhelmed at the Blue Licks, August 19

Preliminary peace treaty signed in Paris, November 30

British evacuate Charleston, December 14

1783 Congress proclaims cessation of hostilities, April 19

Final peace treaty signed, September 3

British evacuate New York City, November 25

Washington retires from command, December 23

Index

221

Index

Index

Index

THE CHICAGO HISTORY OF AMERICAN CIVILIZATION

Daniel J. Boorstin, Editor

Edmund S. Morgan, *The Birth of the Republic: 1763–89*

Marcus Cunliffe, *The Nation Takes Shape: 1789–1837*

*Elbert B. Smith, *The Death of Slavery: 1837–65*

John Hope Franklin, *Reconstruction: After the Civil War*

Samuel P. Hays, *The Response to Industrialism: 1885–1914*

William E. Leuchtenburg, *The Perils of Prosperity: 1914–32*

Dexter Perkins, *The New Age of Franklin Roosevelt: 1932–45*

Herbert Agar, *The Price of Power: America since 1945*

* * *

Robert H. Bremner, *American Philanthropy*

Harry L. Coles, *The War of 1812*

Richard M. Dorson, *American Folklore*

John Tracy Ellis, *American Catholicism*

Nathan Glazer, *American Judaism*

William T. Hagan, *American Indians*

Winthrop S. Hudson, *American Protestantism*

Maldwyn Allen Jones, *American Immigration*

Robert G. McCloskey, *The American Supreme Court*

Howard H. Peckham, *The War for Independence: A Military History*

Howard H. Peckham, *The Colonial Wars: 1689–1762*

Henry Pelling, *American Labor*

*John B. Rae, *The American Automobile: A Brief History*

Charles P. Roland, *The Confederacy*

Otis A. Singletary, *The Mexican War*

John F. Stover, *American Railroads*

*Bernard A. Weisberger, *The American Newspaperman*

* Available in cloth only. All other books published in both cloth and paperback editions.